Real Life Financial Planning
with Case Studies
for Veterinarians

Todd D. Bramson, CFP®, CLU, ChFC

with Contributing Author
Darby L. Affeldt, DVM
Financial Advisor

Published via CreateSpace
ISBN-13: 978-1519398291
ISBN-10: 1519398298

Dedications

This book is dedicated to our spouses, parents, children, siblings, and many friends and relatives. Without the love, support, and guidance of all of these people, we wouldn't have learned the most important lesson of life...

"When all is said and done, it is the quality and depth of relationships and experiences that are the essence of life...not the accumulation of material possessions."

Thank You

We extend a special thank you to...

...our clients who have trusted us with their financial decisions

...our support staff who help us manage a complex business

...our business partners

...each other for the valuable input on this book

Additional books in the *Real Life* book series

Real Life Financial Planning
(Fourth printing)

Real Life Financial Planning for Young Dentists
(Third printing)

Real Life Financial Planning for the High Income Specialist

Real Life Financial Planning for Young Lawyers

Real Life Financial Planning with Case Studies
(featuring Langdon Ford Financial)

Real Life Money Management for Pharmacists

Real Life Financial Planning for the New Physician
(Third printing)

Real Life Financial Planning for Physicians

Real Life Financial Planning for the Medical Professional

Real Life Financial Planning with Case Studies for Women

Real Life Financial Planning for the Student-Athlete

Real Life Financial Planning with Case Studies for Physicians

Real Life Financial Planning
with Case Studies for Veterinarians

CONTENTS

Preface

I have gained wisdom, strength of character, integrity, empathy, and the value of giving by my parents' example. Unfortunately, my father passed away very suddenly at the age of forty-five, when I was just sixteen. It was three weeks from the day he discovered a few black and blue marks on his arms to the day he died of acute leukemia. In this short time, we never had a chance to talk about the future, although I feel his guidance through my conscience and in the wisdom of others, including my mother.

It is interesting how the experiences of childhood, both good and bad, mold the path we follow as adults. My dad did not have much life insurance, or any established relationships with trusted advisors. When he died, my mother was lost financially. She was given very poor financial advice, and the small amount of life insurance she had was lost in an unsuitable and inappropriate investment. My family's misfortune defined my passion. It was through this unfortunate situation that I became empowered. My mission has remained intact for over twenty-five years as I decided this would never happen to my family or anyone who entrusted me with their important financial decisions.

Due to our significant financial crisis, I became eligible for an Evans Scholarship. In the early 1930s, Chick Evans became a nationally ranked golfer and started a college scholarship program with his earnings instead of turning pro. This scholarship has now grown to the largest privately funded scholarship in the country. There are over 920 students currently benefiting from it, as well as over 10,000 alumni. His vision and generosity has been an inspiration to me.

With that in mind, these books are my benevolence. I am now in the fortunate position of being able to give back. Some of the proceeds from this book will be given to charity, including the Evans Scholars Foundation, Breakfast Optimist Foundation, MDRT Foundation, Madison Community Foundation, Leukemia

Society, and many others. I am interested in "partnering" with other charities to help in their fundraising efforts, and I encourage you to contact me to discuss those possibilities.

I'd like to share a proverb containing some valuable wisdom and insight:

He (or She!) who knows, and knows he knows, is wise;
Follow him.
He who knows, but knows not that he knows, is asleep;
Awaken him.
He who knows not, and knows he does not know, is simple;
Teach him.
He who knows not, but does not know that he knows not, is dangerous;
Avoid him.

I believe it's our mission in life to listen to and learn from, or **follow**, those who fall into the first category. But it is also our mission to take our unique gifts and make them available to those who are asleep or simple by **awakening** and **teaching** them. Also, time is too precious to spend with those who are dangerous. **Avoid** and minimize the amount of time you spend with people who fall into this category, and your enjoyment of life will multiply. We all have unique gifts and abilities, and to the extent that our lives overlap and intertwine, we can all grow together carrying out our unique visions.

I am particularly grateful for the time, energy, and wisdom that Darby has put into this book. This text is much more thorough and helpful with her input. The individual case studies in Chapter 10 provide an excellent summary and reference point for many situations veterinarians face. It is my hope that this book will educate, motivate, and help you achieve all of your personal and financial goals.

Todd D. Bramson
December 2015

Tax Disclosure

This information is a general discussion of the relevant federal tax laws. It is not intended for, nor can it be used by any taxpayer for the purpose of, avoiding federal tax penalties. This information is provided to support the promotion or marketing of ideas that may benefit a taxpayer. Taxpayers should seek the advice of their own tax and legal advisors regarding any tax and legal issues applicable to their specific circumstances.

Todd Bramson and Darby Affeldt offer securities and investment advisory services, including Fee-based Financial Planning, through Securian Financial Services, Inc. and CRI Securities, LLC., affiliates and members FINRA/SIPC. Separate from the financial plan and our role as financial planner, we may recommend the purchase of specific investment or insurance products or accounts. These product recommendations are not part of the financial plan and you are under no obligation to follow them.

1

The Basic Questions

Why the Title "Real Life Financial Planning with case studies for Veterinarians?"

Collectively, we have spent over thirty years working directly with individuals on their financial plans and financial planning questions. There is so much information to be found...but sometimes not much wisdom. Hopefully this book summarizes the wisdom we have learned and shared with our veterinarian clients in individual meetings throughout the years. *Real Life Financial Planning with Case Studies for Veterinarians* is simply a practical method of understanding, organizing, and prioritizing financial decisions.

Most financial planning publications and financial plans themselves assume everyone lives a long, healthy life and saves a good portion of their income in quality investments that always do well. This book addresses all of the issues that happen in real life, and I hope you take the time to read this and work with a trained professional to develop a financial plan that meets *your* goals and objectives.

Why Is There an Ever-Increasing Number of Financial Planning Books on the Market Today?

Because there is an ever-increasing need to get educated.

- Few parents openly discuss financial matters with their children while they're growing up.

- Most veterinarians have spent almost 20,000 hours educating themselves on their specialty and not more than five to ten for personal financial planning, if that!
- Most veterinarians today begin their professional life already *in the red*. The average veterinarian finishes their training with over $150,000 in debt. (And in some cases, much more!)
- Veterinarians live high-pressure, busy lifestyles that do not allow much free time to try to learn about all of the options they have.

These unfortunate facts mean there are far too many veterinarians today who are ill equipped to deal with the practical and fundamental necessities of planning for a secure and independent financial life.

Times have changed. Today, more than ever, your financial future needs you. Long gone are the days when you could rely on your veterinary practice to provide you with a retirement plan that covers all of your needs. This is even more evident as we learn that some of America's largest companies report that their pension plans are underfunded. With all the health care changes, it is more apparent than ever that you should take charge of your own financial security.

Certainly the government can't assure you of a reasonable retirement after a lifetime of Social Security contributions. Of course, Social Security was never designed to be the primary income for retirees. In addition, financial products have become increasingly complex, and we are continually inundated with confusing financial information.

These facts aren't meant to stress you out, but to wake you up to the financial reality of America today. It's not simply a matter of whether you will be able to retire rich, but whether you will simply be able to sustain your current lifestyle for the rest of your life.

Don't wait another day. This book is meant to give you an introduction into the often-intimidating world of financial planning. You will learn of the varieties of investments and insurance options. You will begin to understand some terminology, and get advice on where to go next, whether you intend to go the road alone or get some help along the way. Best of all, you will climb the pyramid of financial success.

Financial success isn't, as most people might suspect, the ability to make one or two decisions that turn a buck into a million. Rather, financial success is the result of many small but sound decisions that, when compounded, add up to substantial financial security.

You are in complete control. Or at least you should be. When it comes to spending and saving, investing and paying taxes, many may offer good advice, but you're the only one who can do anything about it. Maybe you're a chronic shopper. Maybe you're unsure of your investment options and how to prioritize them. Maybe you don't have a clue where your paycheck goes each month. In any case, if you're reading this book, you already understand the importance of getting your future under control, and that's the crucial first step to financial freedom.

Who Needs a Financial Planner?

Financial independence and the accumulation of wealth are no accident. Granted, it's not possible to plan for every single event in life, but even tragedy can feel more manageable when you are financially prepared for it. *If you're like most veterinarians, you probably spend more time planning for a vacation than for your entire financial future!* Whether it's preparing for the future, securing yourself and your family against tragedy, or planning for the good times, your money deserves your undivided attention.

Car accidents, marriage, divorce, kids, corporate downsizing, disability, death, and retirement, for better or worse, are the realities of life. Planning for any circumstance, both happy and sad, may seem like a burden right now, but the right planning will rescue you when (not if) unforeseen circumstances arise. Sometimes, solid planning can even turn otherwise bad fortune into good—maybe that downsizing could lead to a better job, or the divorce to a healthier situation, or the large credit card bill finally gives you the motivation to curb your spending and live on a budget.

The truth is, we all need to plan for our financial futures. So the question is not whether to plan, but how to go about making a plan, and whether we need a professional to help. The information age has complicated the field of financial planning. It is interesting to consider that twenty years ago financial news may have made top headlines two or three times throughout the year when the stock market would do particularly poorly or well, or if there was some other major economic news. Today, however, we have news programs dedicated to nothing else 24-7, and the number of financial headlines in the daily papers can be overwhelming. Still, there is a big difference between information and wisdom, and that's where the insight of a trusted professional can help.

Several situations that may call for a financial planner's expertise are:

- *You are a veterinarian without much spare time.* If you're working for a large clinic or hospital, they may provide the groundwork for investing wisely for the long term, but even the best can't take into consideration the special circumstances of each individual or family. In this case, a financial planner can save you a bit of your most precious commodity—time.
- *You are easily bored or overwhelmed by financial questions.* If, for example, preparing a budget is such a nuisance that you can't even imagine having to sort through anything more complex, like insurance options, trends in mutual funds, or

the stock market, then hiring a financial planner may be money well spent for greater peace of mind.

- *You are considering a complicated set of employee benefits in combination with personally owned insurance and investments.* You certainly don't want a new employer (or an existing employer who has changed their benefit structure) to conflict or overlap with your current investments. Such gaps or possible duplications should be examined thoroughly.

- *You are recently divorced or have lost a spouse who had previously been the one handling financial affairs for the household.* As if dealing with the trauma of divorce or death is not enough, being thrust into unknown financial waters without a trusted advisor can make you feel like you're trying to stay afloat with bricks chained to your ankles.

- *You have recently finished veterinary school, an internship or your residency and are suddenly thrust into making many important and critical decisions.* The saying "An ounce of prevention beats a pound of cure" is an important one in the world of financial planning. Seemingly insurmountable debt plagues the future of many veterinarians. Learning to budget properly, to choose from insurance options, and to make wise investments are necessary life skills. Getting professional advice now beats paying for costly mistakes later.

- *You are running or will be starting your own practice.* In this case, you most likely have to "wear many hats" as an entrepreneur. You are in manufacturing, sales, marketing, accounting, and customer servicing, personnel, and oh yeah…practicing medicine and probably don't have time to investigate or be aware of the many planning options available to you for you and your employees. A financial planner can help you sort through the many issues facing you.

As much as some of us would like to leave it all up to a professional, it's crucial that you understand the basics. A financial advisor is someone there to educate and advise you and assist you in taking action to develop a plan, but ultimately the final decisions are yours. A good financial planner will educate you as to the options you face, acting as a teacher, so that you understand all of the relevant issues. Then you can work together to create a plan, and monitor it over the years. A successful financial plan is an ongoing process that stays up to date with your situation.

There are many sides to most issues. The topic doesn't matter, whether it's religion, politics, stocks, insurance, sales loads, or how to finance your house…just to name a few. There are always many individual considerations, and the correct solution depends on a variety of factors. We are leery of advice that suggests you should "always" do this or "never" do that. We believe life is far more gray than it is black and white.

We are not the first to say this, and we certainly won't be the last: "It is crucial to trust your own judgment and instincts before taking action, no matter how good someone makes their argument." The best way to gain confidence in your own better judgment is to educate yourself on the topic at hand.

With that in mind, in this book, you'll find general guidance to the most important financial questions facing everyone:

- How much money should I have in emergency reserves?
- In which order should I go about paying off my debts?
- Which is the right kind of insurance for me, and how much do I need?
- What are the most common financial mistakes people make?

- When should I maximize contributions to retirement plans?
- What cash flow issues should I consider when buying a house?

...and many more!

If you don't know the answers yet, don't worry. Just keep reading, because you're about to find out.

2

Where Do I Start?

Your Net Worth Statement

The starting point of any financial plan is to figure out your current net worth. This is a snapshot of what you are worth at an exact point in time. To determine your net worth, you simply add up all of your assets and subtract all of your liabilities (debts). Sometimes, when you are just starting out, the net worth is actually a negative number because the liabilities exceed the assets.

To measure your financial progress, it is important to know your net worth. Many people measure their financial progress by how much money they have in the bank. In reality, as the value of your assets go up, such as a house, business, or investments, and as you pay debts down, your net worth may be increasing more dramatically than you think. The most important way to measure financial progress is to calculate your net worth regularly.

Don't panic! Here's where we have to get just a bit technical. Before you shake your head and think, "Whoa, this looks way too involved for me," just try taking it one step at a time, following the chart and example on page 21. After you learn how to do it once, it'll be just like riding a bike.

In simple terms, what would you be worth if you sold everything you owned and turned it into cash, then paid off all your debts? If this is the first time you're preparing a net worth statement, it's also a good idea to try to estimate what you think your net worth has been over the last few years. Hopefully you will be pleasantly surprised at the progress you've made.

There are several categories within the net worth statement.

Fixed assets is the first category. Fixed assets are those assets that do not have a risk of a loss of principal. These would include the most conservative accounts you can invest in. A few examples would be checking and savings accounts, bank-issued money market accounts, certificates of deposit, T-bills, EE savings bonds, and whole life (non-variable) insurance cash values. These would be assets you have access to in an emergency. They are available now, and therefore are considered liquid.

Variable assets include most other financial assets. Examples include stocks, bonds, mutual funds, retirement plans, or any investment where the principal can fluctuate. Besides that, there is a potential for a higher overall rate of return on these assets (with greater return potential), and they are useful for the income and growth components of your longer-term financial planning. Please know that investments will fluctuate and, when redeemed, may be worth more or less than when originally invested.

Your *personal and other assets* would include tangible assets such as your house, personal or business property, and vehicles. Other tangible assets, such as a stereo, computer, or camera, would also be included here.

Don't get too bogged down trying to establish a value for every piece of personal property. You may already have that information available from your homeowner's or renter's insurance policies, but if not, a rough estimate will work just fine. The main reason for gathering this information is to have an estimate so you can monitor trends. This way, when you are reviewing your net worth after some time, you will be able to track how this category has changed or account for some of the money you spent.

Net Worth Statement

Fixed Assets:

Savings Account:	$5,000
Checking Account:	$3,000
Certificate of Deposit:	$2,000
Total Fixed Assets:	**$10,000**

Invested Assets:

IRA:	$3,000
Mutual Funds:	$5,000
Individual Stocks:	$2,000
Variable Life Cash Value:	$4,000
401k Balance:	$20,000
Total Invested Assets:	**$34,000**

Other Assets:

Home:	$200,000
Vehicle:	$20,000
Personal Property	$20,000
Total Other Assets:	**$240,000**
Total Assets:	**$284,000**

Liabilities:

Mortgage:	$160,000
Home Equity Line of Credit:	$5,000
Vehicle Loan:	$10,000
Credit Cards:	$2,000
Total Liabilities:	**$177,000**

NET WORTH (Assets minus Liabilities):   **$107,000**

*Tip: Record a video or take photos of each room in your house, including closets and the garage. In the event of a loss, it will be much easier to remember for insurance company's reporting purposes.

For your liabilities, list the amount you owe if you could pay off the amount today, not the total of the payments over time, which would include interest. Subtract your total liabilities from your assets to arrive at your net worth. If you're like many people, this can be a sobering experience. Don't forget to include all loans, like mortgages, auto loans, credit cards, student loans, personal debts, and consumer debt.

Don't feel too upset if you learn your net worth is negative. It is very common for a young veterinarian to have a negative net worth because of their student loans. However, remember that your education is an asset, and student loans are an investment in your financial future.

If you fit into the negative net worth category, your first financial goal is to get your new worth back to zero. For you, it is especially important to establish a financial plan and get control of your financial life as soon as possible. But instead of dreading the process, have some fun with it. I suggest that clients throw themselves an "I'm Worthless Party" after they've worked hard to achieve their "$0" net worth. (Just don't put the party on a credit card you can't pay off next month!)

Ignore the urge to put your head in the sand, thinking you have no power over the situation. *You are not alone, and there's no reason to be embarrassed.* To prove it, you can take a look at our government. Their high federal deficit sets a dangerous precedent not only for our culture, but also the world's economy. No matter how big your debt problem, it looks relatively small in this light!

Simply make up your mind now to reverse the situation, and be proud that you're taking the right steps. The obvious way to improve your net worth is to decrease your spending and/or increase your income and savings. Begin by taking a serious look at your spending habits, and make sure you are doing everything you can to achieve, first a zero, and eventually a positive net worth. Getting yourself back to financial stability may feel like a long and lonely road, but with the help of a financial planner, you at least don't have to feel like you're going at it alone. Or why not "buddy up" like people do when they work out. Find a friend who is also motivated to get their financial act in order, and educate yourselves and build your net worth together. After a while, being frugal, saving and investing, and getting on top of your finances becomes addicting.

The Millionaire Next Door by Thomas Stanley outlines some benchmark figures for what your net worth should be at any given time, age, or stage in life. I'd encourage you to read that book for an in-depth study of very successful people. Your net worth represents your financial security and, ultimately, financial independence. So of course, the closer you are to retirement, the higher your net worth should be. A successful financial plan achieves one's maximum net worth, works under the most difficult circumstances, and maximizes the enjoyment of your wealth. It will also be important to insure yourself against unforeseen tragedies and to consider whether you want to leave an inheritance to your family or your favorite charity, creating a legacy that lives on forever.

In summary, the most critical starting point to a financial plan is evaluating your net worth. Then, on a periodic basis, you can compare the results in order to establish trends and measure improvement. A convenient time to do this is once a year when you're doing your taxes. This way, all the paperwork is readily available and you're focused on your annual earnings and expenditures anyway. Keep all the financial records together from each year's tax forms and net worth calculations for easy reference.

Your Budget

After calculating your net worth, you'll want to look at your monthly budget and define exactly where your money is being spent. The categories of the monthly budget should also include any deductions from your paycheck, like state and federal income taxes, Social Security, and employee benefits. Once you have your take-home pay, you should deduct all of the fixed expenses and the estimated variable expenses.

Are you unable to account for where a large portion of your money goes? This is the case for many people. To overcome it, try a few of the following tips:

- Carry a pocket calendar with you for three months, and record every cent you spend, no matter if it's for a candy bar or a cup of coffee, or the mortgage and car payment. Then tally it up and categorize it at the end of each month. (Some software programs, like *Quicken*, make this very easy. Well...maybe not easy, but at least helpful. This process takes some time, but is well worth it if you are a spender.)

- Vow to go back to the days of cash-only transactions. For everything other than your large monthly payments (and even those, if you want to get really serious), stop using your debit and credit cards or writing checks for day-to-day expenditures like groceries, drugstore items, clothing, and so on. It feels much different when you have to shell out $50 cash for a purchase rather than handing over a piece of plastic.

- If cash is a hassle to replenish or carry around, and you can stay *extremely disciplined* and commit to pay off your balance in full each month, then consider a rewards credit card. This can be helpful to track every cent you spend while simultaneously earning cash back or even free travel. Use the card to buy even the smallest items or pay utility bills, for example—as long as the vendor doesn't charge a fee, of course! It is well worth it to ask if you can use a credit card to pay and amazing how quickly rewards add up! If you decide to use this strategy, use the "cash-only" mentality while making purchases and ask yourself before the card is brandished to the cashier "will I be able to pay this off when the bill comes?". If not, don't buy it.

- Treat your savings account or investment amount as a bill you pay out every month like any other. Experience has shown that if you don't get in the habit of saving money on a regular basis, either through a payroll deduction or an automatic withdrawal from your checking account, the money you intended to go toward savings or investments is mysteriously spent elsewhere.

How quickly you can move toward financial security depends on how motivated you are to save money. It's not easy for Americans to live on less than their income, considering our shopping and credit-loving culture. However, if you start early enough, saving 15 percent of your gross income will typically be enough to help keep you safe from financial worries later on. If you are getting a later start, you may need to be living on 75 to 80 percent of your income and saving 20 to 25 percent!

Keep in mind that saving or investing 15 percent means you are able to live on 85 percent of your income. As elementary as this may sound, the significance is critical. In later years, this savings could accumulate to a substantial sum if invested properly. Also, it will teach you how to live below your means—a financial goal that seemingly every expert agrees upon, but few Americans live by.

3

The Pyramid

If you take a jigsaw puzzle and dumped all the pieces on the table, it is initially a daunting task to begin to put the puzzle together. Take a puzzle piece out of the pile at random, and it's hard to know where that piece fits into the big picture. It is much easier to put the puzzle together if you have a picture of what the scene will look like once completed. So you look at the picture on the box to give you a guide to what the puzzle looks like when completed. I designed the pyramid as a method of seeing how a properly designed financial plan looks when it is put together correctly. Once you understand that, specific decisions are easier because everything is in perspective.

The pyramid is a method of explaining the financial planning concept by categorizing your financial plan into stages. Of course, individual goals, habits, accomplishments, and so on are all unique, but most people share the same fundamental life stages. As a simple method of efficiently organizing your financial life, the pyramid represents the key to financial independence, and demonstrates the basic goal of increasing your assets and reducing your debt in order to have enough money invested to retire comfortably. Individuals may place more or less importance on one section of the pyramid than another, which is perfectly acceptable.

Without a doubt, organizing your finances in order to build a solid base is the first step. If you do this, you may be subjecting your financial situation to undue risk, which will cause problems later on. On the other hand, it's also important not to place too much emphasis on only one stage, neglecting the overall balance. This could be a sign of being overly conservative. As an example, not taking advantage of higher potential returns in equity (stock) investments may mean losing your purchasing power in the long run, because the dollars may be worth less due to the effects of taxes and inflation.

It is very important to try to accomplish a lifelong financial balance. You certainly don't want to get to the age of sixty-five with a huge amount of money saved up, only to be in poor health and not be able to enjoy it, especially if that means you scrimped and saved your whole life and worked so hard that you didn't enjoy yourself along the way. By the same token, you don't want to be nearing retirement and realize you haven't saved enough and now must take a substantial drop in your standard of living or go back to work to simply survive. The ideal situation would be to retire at the same or a greater standard of living than you were accustomed to in your working years, but not feel at any time that you have greatly sacrificed.

As mentioned in Chapter 2, a fundamental of short- and long-term financial success is living on less than your income. If you can get used to living on 80 to 90 percent of your income, this allows you to commit 10 to 20 percent of your income to your net worth. Initially, this may mean aggressively paying of loans, but over time, the majority of this extra income should be saved. If you are living paycheck to paycheck, is there a way you can decrease your expenses and/or increase your income so you can start building some surplus funds into your monthly budget?

As you can see by the diagram below, there are four main stages to the financial planning pyramid: the *Security and Confidence Stage*, the *Capital Accumulation Stage*, the *Tax-Advantaged Stage*, and the *Speculation Stage*.

Pyramid of Financial Needs

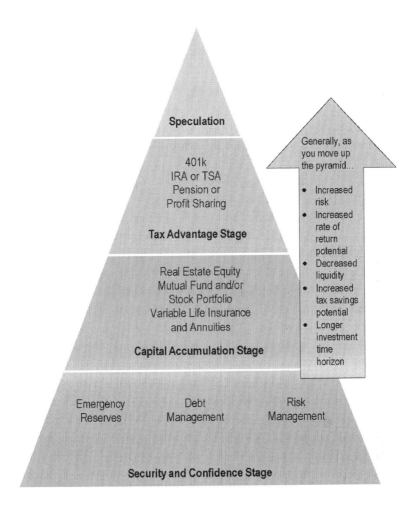

The ideal investment is completely liquid and has lots of tax advantages, a great rate of return, and low risk. If you find an advisor or salesperson claiming to have such an investment, you would be wise to walk, no, run away. This ideal investment does not exist.

Let's use an analogy of spinning plates. If you have ever been to a circus or seen a juggler (the Peking acrobats), you may have seen a performer attempt to spin many plates on top of long sticks…all at the same time. The objective is to take limited energy, and allocate it in such a manner as to keep all the plates spinning. It doesn't do any good to devote a lot of time to one spinning plate while the others are slowing down, wobbling, and falling down. The goal is to keep all the plates spinning!

Your financial plan is on somewhat the same level, with each financial decision representing a different plate. First, you need to find out which plates you want to start spinning, and then direct your dollars to keep them going. You could have several debt reduction plates, some risk management (insurance) plates, retirement and/or college education plates, and so on. Each individual situation is going to be different. Again, there are limited resources that need to be allocated in such a way as to accomplish all of your goals. This is where the advice of a professional and experienced financial advisor can be very valuable. You can call me a financial juggler.

The key financial variables in the pyramid are risk, liquidity, rate of return, and tax advantages. The money in your emergency reserves and at the *Security and Confidence Stage* should be very liquid or accessible. Generally, as you move to higher stages in the pyramid, the less liquid your funds become.

Risk and rate of return tend to go hand in hand. The higher the amount of risk you take, the higher the rate of return potential should be…given time. In the pyramid, typically lower risk and lower rates of return should be at the base of your planning, with risk and rate of return increasing as you move up the pyramid. Historically, stock market and investing returns become less volatile the longer the timeframe that is considered. Keep in mind, however, that past performance is not indicative of future results. Investments will fluctuate and, when redeemed, could be worth more or less than when originally invested.

From a tax standpoint, there are typically not too many tax advantages at the lower level. If you have money in a savings account, that money is generating ordinary income on which you are paying tax, so there are no tax advantages there. On the other hand, when you put money into a qualified retirement plan, the contribution is on a before-tax basis, delaying and deferring the tax to a later date. Under most circumstances, however, you cannot touch the money in your qualified plan until age fifty-nine and a half without paying a 10 percent early withdrawal penalty, plus the income taxes due on that amount. The rule of thumb on tax savings is similar to risk and rate of return. As you move up the pyramid, you'll have greater tax advantages on your investments.

A Discussion of Risk

There is no such thing as a risk-free investment. Even a savings account is not risk-free. Let me explain. Risk is commonly discussed in terms of loss of principal. This is market risk. Most recently, during the recent bear markets of 2000–2001 and 2007–2009 (a period of downturn in the stock market); many investors lost some of the value of their investment if they owned stocks and/or stock mutual funds. There are other forms of risk besides market risk.

Purchasing Power Risk: Another term for this is inflation. If the cost for products and services rises faster than the interest rate being credited on your savings and checking accounts, you are exposed to purchasing power risk. While you don't lose any principal, you are still losing ground relative to inflation. This is a particular problem currently for retirees who have traditionally held CDs (bank certificates of deposit) and lived off the interest each year.

Interest Rate Risk: Bonds and fixed income securities are subject to this risk. Your principal value can decline if interest rates climb quickly. The severity of the loss is often magnified by the duration and/or maturity of the bonds and the credit quality, as well as how quickly interest rates rise. At this time, when interest rates are near forty-year lows, many people who own fixed income securities are unknowingly subjecting their investments to interest rate risk.

Business Risk: This is the risk of losing money due to circumstances out of your control. A business could go bankrupt, and your investment becomes worthless.

Liquidity Risk: This is the risk associated with being invested in real estate, securities, businesses, and other investments where there is sometimes no immediate market for your value. This is problematic if you have a need for cash and you cannot sell or liquidate your shares. You would invest in something like this only if you had sufficient assets available besides this investment.

Regulatory Risk: Investors run the risk that government policy decisions or influences of society as a whole could endanger an investment's value. Environmental and tax legislation can have a dramatic impact on certain investment values, up or down. It is important to note this risk when investing.

Currency Risk: An investment in international securities can be affected by foreign exchange rate changes, political and economic instability, as well as differences in accounting standards.

Asset Protection Risk: This is the risk associated with a loss of net worth due to lawsuits, malpractice claims, and so on. The higher your income and net worth is, the greater the risk. The more complex planning goes beyond the scope of this text and includes titling and ownership issues, legal documents, and so on.

Identity Theft: We are all vulnerable. Identity theft has been the number one consumer complaint to the Federal Trade Commission for the past fifteen years straight, affecting millions of Americans each year and costing billions in dollars and time as victims struggle to put their lives back together. Take steps now to reduce your risk and have professionals help you when victimized.

Diversity Risk: This will be discussed at length later in the book, but allow me to overstate the obvious...DIVERSIFY!

In summary, a properly structured financial plan will balance all of these variables so that you are diversified by asset class, risk levels, tax treatment, and time horizon.

4

The Security and Confidence Stage

This stage is divided into three main sections, with an emphasis on building up emergency reserves, making sure debt is under control, and taking care of risk management (insurance) needs. Each of these factors is equally important. Most people agree on the need to have money accessible for emergencies, to pay their debts, especially on high-interest credit cards, and to be adequately insured. The trick to the individual financial plan is to figure out the appropriate level for each of these.

1. Emergency Reserves

The one constant in life is that there will always be surprises. The purpose of an emergency reserve fund is just what it sounds like—money that is very accessible when you really need it. In fact, Will Rogers once said, "I'm not so much concerned about the rate of return on my money, just the return of it!" The main characteristic of an investment in this category would be money that is liquid, yet invested in more stable investment options so the principal remains intact. The most common mistake people make here is not having adequate reserves or taking undue risk with these funds. This money needs to remain liquid in case of unexpected expenses, like car expenses, home repairs, job loss, or medical emergencies. For most people, the main benefit of having an adequate emergency reserve fund is access to funds when needed. When you are financially prepared for these surprises, they become less stressful and are therefore easier to deal with emotionally. Furthermore, when there is a source of funds for these types of emergencies, you do not have to rely on credit cards or personal unsecured high-interest loans.

As a general rule of thumb, your emergency reserve account would be able to cover at least three months of bills. So, if your monthly expenses are averaging $10,000, your emergency reserve fund should be $30,000. Of course, this is a rough guide, and you may want to consider having a higher emergency reserve if you anticipate a big purchase, such as a car or home. Ideally, you do not want to deplete your emergency reserve completely in order to purchase such items.

It may also be important to consider an *emotional rule of thumb*—at what point would a drop in your emergency reserves make you feel nervous? Or, said another way, what is the minimum level of cash you need to have? This amount differs for everyone, and it should take into consideration the stability of your job, your equity in a home, how large and/or liquid your other investments are, and any large bills or purchases you may be planning. If a large purchase or unexpected expenses do drain your reserves, the emphasis of your financial plan should be to replenish those funds at a higher priority than your other investments.

The typical investments that can be used to hold your emergency reserves would include bank investments, money market funds, and/or insurance cash values. The common theme among these investments is their liquidity and the safety of the principal. If you use a bank for your emergency reserves, typically these funds are in savings accounts and interest-bearing checking accounts, and bank-issued money market accounts.

For safety of principal and liquidity, savings accounts are the most common option, but not necessarily the best. Such accounts are insured, so there is no market risk, but lots of purchasing poser risk. But this also means there is typically a lower yield than other investments.

Another option is a CD (certificate of deposit), with a relatively short maturity. The disadvantage to a CD is that the money is tied up for the length of the guarantee period, and removing the funds sooner will result in a penalty. To avoid this problem, it can make sense to stagger your CD maturities so that you always have some that come due every six months or so. Therefore, you can access it if you need to or reinvest if you don't.

A money market mutual fund is often good choice as an emergency reserve possibility. Many people incorrectly associate the term mutual fund with high risk. However, a mutual fund only has as much risk as the underlying investments it owns. A money market mutual fund pools investors' dollars in the typical mutual fund style, and purchases jumbo CDs through banks, Treasury securities (T-bills), as well as commercial paper. Most money market funds have a check writing privilege, which allows you to write checks against your account, subject to minimums of usually $250 or $500. The rate of return earned on these funds will fluctuate based on the short-term money market, but it is typically competitive with the interest rate at the time.

Investments in a money market fund are neither insured nor guaranteed by the FDIC, or any government agency. Although the fund seeks to preserve the value of your investment at $1.00 per share, it is possible to lose money by investing in the fund. In the fall of 2008, the Reserve Primary Fund did fall to $.97 per share, losing 3 percent of the principal.

Life insurance cash values on permanent policies (i.e., whole life, adjustable life, universal life) can also be important sources of emergency reserve funds. These funds are typically earning a competitive fixed rate of return, and they are accessible. It is usually possible to take out a loan or borrow against your cash value, using it as collateral. Or sometimes you can take an outright withdrawal of this money. Remember, though, that any loans or withdrawals taken will reduce both your policy cash value and death benefit.

A home equity line of credit is another option. If you have equity in your house, and if interest rates are low and these loans are tax-deductible, this option should not be discounted. In fact, in periods of time when interest rates are low, maintaining an open line of credit against your house can be a source of money in an emergency. It could also be used to pay down a high-interest credit card or for a major purchase, like a car. The drawback is that it needs to be paid off when you sell your house, which of course would result in fewer proceeds at closing. This can also happen if the house falls in value. If your house would decline in value, creating less equity, you may have to pay off the home equity line and/or face a higher interest rate on the loan. You should never take home equity and invest in the market. This is a dangerous practice that encompasses too much risk.

2. Debt Management

If you are in the fortunate situation of having no debts, congratulations! If you come from the school of thought that you don't ever want to owe anything to anybody, debt management is not an issue. However, in today's society, this ideology is very uncommon and many people could use some strategies on effectively managing their debt.

Financially, it would make sense to rank all of your debts from highest to lowest interest, paying attention to the after-tax cost of borrowing. Since consumer debt is not tax-deductible, those rates are taken at face value. However, a mortgage or home equity loan is deductible, so the real rate of return is the after-tax cost.

To give another general rule of thumb, credit cards and consumer debt would be the first to pay off, if they have the highest interest rates. Then you would want to work away at the furniture loan, the used car loan, the new car loan, student loans, and finally, the home mortgage. Nowadays there are many credit cards that offer very low interest rates on balance transfers, which can be a temporary solution. But beware that the rate after the introductory period is not actually higher than your current card.

It is also important to look at debt management from a cash flow standpoint as well as an emotional standpoint. With this in mind, it can make sense to pay off a lower-interest loan if it will improve your cash flow dramatically, or if emotionally it is important for you to get it paid off for some other reason. Many people find a sense of satisfaction in paying debts off completely. Once one debt is paid off, take the extra cash and immediately begin paying off another loan more aggressively, so that cash does not get absorbed into the budget.

Check your credit report. It's a good idea to review your credit report every year. The financial information included in this report will have a bearing on whether you can obtain a loan, get auto or home insurance, rent an apartment, or even apply for a job. Contact the credit bureaus and correct any errors you find. We would suggest starting at www.annualcreditreport.com.

3. Risk Management

Protecting yourself against unforeseen catastrophic losses is the third critical area of the base of the pyramid and the *Security and Confidence Stage*. In fact, think of this as a three-legged stool. Kick one leg out, and the stool will not stand. The financial pyramid is just like that.

Important insurance coverage can include health and major medical, auto, disability, long-term care, and homeowners or renters. In many cases, life and/or disability insurance are overlooked. However, these can be very important depending on your personal situation.

The reason for placing risk management at this point is obvious. You need to protect yourself from losses that would create such a hole that you may otherwise never dig yourself out. Then, once you are on your way to financial independence, insurance plays an equally important role in protecting your assets.

While you don't want to have any gaps in your insurance protection, you certainly don't want to overlap or duplicate coverage. The ideal financial plan will have you paying reasonable premium levels while providing maximum protection. Remember, the major role of insurance is to protect against catastrophic losses. A common mistake is trying to insure too many contingencies or not using deductibles to your advantage.

You will want to ask yourself a couple of questions before purchasing insurance:

- Is the premium for this coverage going to dramatically affect my lifestyle?
- If I do not buy this coverage and suffer the losses that would have been covered, would I be in grave financial trouble?

If the answer to the first question is "No" and to the second "Yes," the insurance in question is right for you. If not, reconsider the structure and price of the insurance. Consult an experienced financial professional to help you determine the appropriate levels of coverage and how to structure your insurance within the context of a comprehensive financial plan.

When it comes to life insurance, it is easy to become confused. Some complicated terminology like "term life," "whole life," "universal life," and "variable whole life" may put you off, but by understanding just a few terms and some of the benefits and disadvantages, you will be much more prepared to evaluate the coverage that is best for you. If structured correctly, life insurance can be one of the most versatile and powerful financial tools available. Life insurance products contain fees, such as mortality and expense charges, and may contain restrictions, such as surrender charges.

- *Term Life:* While the premiums are low for the young, the price increases dramatically as you get older. Although young couples with children may find term life insurance to be the only affordable option, it is important to remember that this option brings no investment benefits. To optimize value on the policy, a guaranteed renewal clause allows for renewal to the policy without a medical requalification. Another value-adding option is a clause that allows a conversion from a renewable term policy to a permanent policy without proof of insurability.

- *Whole Life:* The most appealing feature of whole life insurance is its unchanging premium and guaranteed long-term coverage. Also, it builds up a tax-deferred "cash value." The cash value is what the insurer will return on cancellation of the policy. But whole life costs more than term life initially. Some critics believe whole life's cash value grows too slowly and, as an investment option, the buyer is better off buying term insurance and investing the difference in the stock market. The policies' rates of returns today are much more competitive than in the past, and this can be a very viable policy for a portion of your financial plan.

- *Adjustable/Universal Life:* The main feature of this policy is the flexibility in initial design and the ability to change as your needs change. If money gets tight, with this type of policy it's possible to lower the annual premium. You can also increase or decrease the death benefit as your needs change. Typically, increases in death benefit require additional proof of insurability.

- *Variable Life:* The cash values are invested into investment sub-accounts with your choice of the allocation to stocks, bonds, and/or money markets. The policy's cash value can increase if the investments do well. But the opposite could also occur. Look ahead to the next chapter for a more advanced discussion of this type of policy and its benefits and risks.

Disability insurance is one of the most important and overlooked types of insurance coverage.

The odds of a long-term disability (lasting ninety days or longer) are 144 percent greater than death occurring during one's working years. (Source: www.disabilityquotes.com/Occupations/page2.cfm) Financially, a long-term disability is worse than death, because your expenses rise and you are still around.

While many employers provide group disability insurance, the benefits are generally 60 percent of one's income and taxable. The net effect is that only 40 to 45 percent of your income is protected. If the group policy is not portable, or you would like more of your income protected than 60 percent, you should obtain an individual policy. Early in your career, the only way to guarantee your income will not stop if something happens to your ability to earn an income is to insure yourself with a quality occupation-specific disability insurance policy. By occupation-specific, this means if you cannot perform the duties of your specialty, you will be compensated

As your assets grow, it is wise to expand your umbrella liability insurance coverage. The limits built into most homeowners and auto policies are minimal. This coverage actually protects your assets in the event that you or a family member cause harm due to your negligence. In addition, be sure to ask your agent for excess umbrella liability coverage for uninsured/underinsured motorists. This coverage protects you and your family for negligent acts caused by others.

You should also review you overall financial plan to see what assets are at risk in the event of a lawsuit. Unfortunately, we live in a society where successful or wealthy people are targeted for lawsuits more than other groups.

Professional Liability insurance should be reviewed periodically whether you are an employee of a large group or practicing in a smaller practice. At a minimum, make sure you have at least the average amount of coverage recommended for general DVM's or your particular specialty. It is also helpful to know whether you have an occurrence or claims made policy. An occurrence policy covers you if your policy was paid up at the time the incident at issue occurred. A claims made policy covers you only if you have a policy in place when the incident occurred and when you are sued.

Remember, you get what you pay for. Searching the Internet for the cheapest insurance policy often results in coverage that will not protect you and your family adequately. A competent insurance agent or financial planner can provide a valuable service, and should be used. They can be the best resource in helping you to select adequate coverage at appropriate prices, and at claim time they can help you decipher the paperwork. Choosing someone you trust, especially someone who comes recommended from a reliable source, will prove invaluable. Also, there may be some other aspects of your overall financial plan that, if reworked, can help you maximize your insurance protection, while building wealth for the future using better strategies than you were aware of

In many cases, insurance is thought of as a "necessary evil." You have to have it, but it only benefits you if you have a claim. We look at the insurance coverage we own as a valuable part of an overall comprehensive financial plan. The peace of mind we have by knowing our families and properties are covered is worth a lot. In addition, we can be more aggressive with our other savings and investments, because we know our risk management needs are taken care of.

Looking back to the Middle Ages, we get a glimpse of the importance of insurance. People of wealth built fabulous castles and filled them with treasures. They always devoted significant resources to protecting those assets in the form of an army, a moat, and so on. In a sense, that was an early form of an insurance policy. So as you continue to build your net worth, you should review and update your insurance to be sure you are maximizing your coverage and protecting you and your family and your wealth.

5

The Capital Accumulation Stage

This stage represents a large amount of assets you will build up over your lifetime. The assets that tend to comprise this stage are quite varied. Some of the investments include individual stocks and bonds, mutual funds, variable life insurance cash values, and equity in real estate or in a business. Aside from the equity you build into your retirement plan, the majority of your financial independence will come from these investments. While these assets can also serve as emergency reserves, the investment horizon is usually five years or longer.

Keep in mind that all investments have risk. However, there are varying degrees and types of risk. The risk most often associated with an investment involves a fluctuating principal or a sudden depreciation in the stock market, as in October 1987 or the bear markets of 2000–2002 and 2007–2009. A corporate bond or government security holds the risk of loss of principal due to an increase in interest rates. Even a relatively stable investment such as a money market fund has, in addition to market risk, purchasing power risk, because after taxes and inflation are figured in, your dollars could be worth less than when you originally invested. A summary of the types of risk is found towards the end of Chapter 3.

Saving money is one of the most important criteria in assuring financial success. Get in the habit now of saving between 10 and 20 percent of your gross income (10 percent if you are starting when you are in your mid-twenties, and 20 percent if you are over age forty). By living below your total income, even to this small degree, not only will your money be worth more in the long run by wisely investing it, but you will also cultivate a responsible attitude toward your money. Keeping up with the Joneses has become a national epidemic. But the real truth is that the millionaires next door don't concern themselves with flaunting their wealth, which explains why they are wealthy. Some of the financial ideas and products that belong in the *Capital Accumulation Stage* are discussed here.

Variable life policies are becoming increasingly popular. Because of their unique investment opportunities, their tax deferral potential, and their return potential, this new type of insurance policy should be examined by anyone who is investing money at the *Capital Accumulation Stage*. Such policies allow an individual to purchase a single financial instrument providing for both life insurance and long-term accumulation goals. Obviously, your level of insurance needs and wants has a large bearing on how the policy is structured, and it's important to carefully structure loans and withdrawals to avoid negative income tax results. Please keep in mind that the primary reasons to purchase a life insurance product is for the death benefit. Investments will fluctuate, and the cash values available for loans, withdrawals, or redemptions may be worth more or less than originally invested. Life insurance products contain fees, such as mortality and expense charges, and may contain restrictions, such as surrender charges. Policy loans and withdrawals may create an adverse tax result in the event of a lapse or policy surrender, and will reduce both the cash value and death benefit.

For many Americans, one of the most substantial forms of saving is simply making a monthly payment on your home. Generally speaking, real estate has long been a favorite investment tool for its tax benefits and as a buffer against inflation. Although there can be significant investment benefits in the long term, buying real estate is not without its risks. Deflation or negative market movement may decrease property values, or suspected long-term growth in a given area may not occur. Changes in tax law may reduce or eliminate anticipated tax benefits. Also, real estate is not liquid, so the necessity of a quick sale may require a substantial reduction in price.

The terms "stock" or "share" both refer to a partial ownership interest in a corporation, or equity. As a stockholder, you'll be able to vote for the company's board of directors, and receive information on the firm's activities and business results. You may share in "dividends" or current profits.

Investors typically buy and hold stock for its long-term growth potential. Stocks with a history of regular dividends are often held for both income and growth. As the long-term growth of a company cannot be predicted, the short-term market value of the company's stock will fluctuate up and down. If your financial need or your fear causes you to sell when the market is "down" (also called a "bear market"), a capital loss can result. If the market is "up" (also called a "bull market"), the investor can realize a capital gain when selling.

While stocks represent ownership in a business, bonds are debt issued by institutions such as the federal government, corporations, and state and local governments. At the bonds' "maturity," the principal amount will be returned. In the meantime, bondholders receive interest. When first issued, a bond will have a specified interest rate, or "yield." If a bond is traded on a public exchange, the market price will fluctuate, generally with changes in interest rates.

Using a diversified mutual fund is an excellent way to help manage your risk, because you are diversifying through a number of stocks. A properly designed mutual fund portfolio is generally the most appropriate method of accumulating wealth at this point in the financial pyramid. Some funds have higher market risk, meaning they can fluctuate quite dramatically. Past experience shows that funds that have the most risk have upside and downside potential that needs to be carefully considered. Funds with lower market risk often have inflation risk. These funds usually produce lower returns that may not keep up with inflation.

If your investment horizon is relatively short (up to five years), a more conservatively balanced fund, equity income fund, or even a medium-term corporate bond or government securities fund will likely be the most appropriate. When your investment horizon is longer, growth-oriented stock funds are generally going to be the best choice. Again, each circumstance is different, and the advice of a competent professional will be valuable. Most firms have a short investment attitude questionnaire you can answer to help you determine the appropriate asset allocation strategy that meets your needs.

Diversify! Diversify! Diversify! Nothing else will be as crucial to your portfolio as diversifying and having a long-term vision. It's important to diversify not only by asset class, but also by tax treatment and time horizon. We all know the proverb "Don't put all your eggs in one basket." Well, take it to the extreme—don't put all the baskets on the same truck, and don't drive all the trucks down the same road! It's not necessary to look too far back to recall the faddish investing in technology and start-up companies of the late 1990s. Too many investors lost significant wealth when the overvalued stocks plunged, and those eager investors expecting big returns were left with substantial losses.

Sometimes misunderstood, the main goal of diversification is not to maximize your return, but to minimize your risk and lower your volatility. The basic premise is that there is as much risk in being out of the market when it goes up as being in the market when it goes down, especially for your long-term money. As an example, take the period between 1926 and 1995, a period of 840 months. If you were out of the market during the thirty top-performing months—about 3.6 percent of the time—you would have ended up with a return similar to Treasury bills! While diversification does not guarantee against loss, it is a method used to manage risk.

Some additional strategies to employ when investing include dollar cost averaging and portfolio rebalancing. Dollar cost averaging is the process of investing a fixed amount of money each month (or quarter, or year) without worrying about whether the market is up or down. When it is down, you will buy more shares, bringing your average share price down. Over time, besides the element of forced savings, you will hopefully see returns you are happy with. Dollar cost averaging does not assure a profit, nor does it protect against loss in declining markets. This investment strategy requires regular investments regardless of the fluctuating price of the investment. You should consider your financial ability to continue investing through periods of low price levels.

When there is a large amount of money to invest, coming up with an investment policy and adhering to it is a must. Once an overall asset allocation mix is chosen based on your goals and objectives, stick to it and change only if there are significant changes in the economy, the portfolio, and/or your goals and objectives. Then, on a regular basis, either quarterly, semiannually, or annually, rebalance the portfolio back to the asset allocation you started with. With this strategy, your investment mix does not get skewed towards more or less risk and volatility. Many current portfolio managers have the capability of providing this rebalancing process on an automatic basis.

A well-balanced portfolio is properly diversified by the following asset decisions:

- Growth stocks: large, medium, and small[1]
- Value stocks: large, medium, and small
- International stocks: developed countries, emerging markets[2]

---

[1] Investments in smaller company and micro-cap stocks generally carry a higher level of volatility and risk over the short term.

- Fixed income: corporate bonds, government bonds, high yield bonds[4]
- Real estate: real property, low correlation with stocks[3]

There are many good resources to turn to that will help you take this process much further than the scope of this book. Some of those are found in Chapter 10. I think some of the best information can come from a competent and qualified financial advisor who will listen to you and develop a plan that meets your needs.

In general, a higher investment risk is best for those who:
- Can accept short-term losses
- Believe gains will offset losses over the long run
- Will not leave the investment if one or two bad years occur
- Have a long investment time horizon

The best way to learn sound market advice is to listen to the experts. The following quotes from mutual fund leaders all stress the futility of market timing:

Peter Lynch: *"My single-most important piece of investment advice is to ignore the short-term fluctuations of the market. From one year to the next, the stock market is a coin flip. It can go up or down. The real money in stocks is made in the third, fourth, and fifth year of your investments, because you are participating in a company's earnings, which grow over time."*

Warren Buffet: *"I do not have, never have had, and never will have an opinion where the stock market will be a year from now."*

---

[2] Investment risks associated with international investing, in addition to other risks, include currency fluctuations, political and economic instability, and differences in accounting standards.

[3] Investment risks associated with investing in the real estate fund/portfolio, in addition to other risks, include rental income fluctuation, depreciation, property tax value changes, and differences in real estate market values.

[4] Fixed income securities are subject to credit and interest rate risk and, as such, their value generally will fall as interest rates rise.

Sir John Templeton: *"Ignore fluctuations. Do not try to outguess the stock market. Buy a quality portfolio, and invest for the long term."*

So, to drive it home, invest for the long term and be patient!

Variable life insurance, variable annuities, and mutual funds are sold only by prospectus. The prospectus contains important information about the product's charges and expenses, as well as the risks and other information associated with the product. You should carefully consider the risks and investment charges of a specific product before investing. You should always read the prospectus carefully before investing.

6

The Tax-Advantaged Stage

The focus of this stage is to try to significantly delay, reduce, and/or minimize the impact of taxes on your financial picture. Why? To accumulate and create the highest net worth you possibly can. One method of delaying the tax involves investing dollars into qualified retirement plans. This means the dollars are made on a before-tax (qualified) basis. Again, the taxes are not eliminated. They are just deferred until the funds are withdrawn. These plans include individual retirement accounts (IRAs), simplified employee pensions (SEPs), tax-sheltered annuities (TSAs), pension and profit-sharing plans, 401k plans, and so on.

The main advantage behind these plans is that the government has given you a significant motivation to save money because your taxable income is reduced dollar for dollar by the contribution, which will then defer anywhere from 10 to 35 percent of the deposit in taxes. In other words, your adjusted gross income is less, which means your taxable income is reduced. While these accounts are good places to defer and delay the tax liability during your working years, they present some problems at retirement because of the tax due then. And transferring qualified assets to heirs can present some tax nightmares if not handled carefully.

The general principal here is to save money into these plans when you are in a higher tax bracket, and withdraw the funds at retirement when you are in a lower tax bracket. We do see some problems, though. In some cases, when a person is early in their career and the income and tax bracket is low, it doesn't make any sense to put a lot of money into an IRA or 401k. Why defer money when you are in the lowest tax bracket you may ever be in? Instead, you may want to contribute to the 401k just up to where the employer matches those funds, but then again, only if you plan to be at that job for a few years to become vested (the employer's matching funds are yours if you are vested when you leave), and have taken care of the *Security and Confidence Stage* of your financial plan.

The reason the *Tax-Advantaged Stage* belongs above the *Capital Accumulation Stage* and *Security and Confidence Stage* of the pyramid is because the money deposited into these plans is normally not available until you reach the age of fifty-nine and a half. (There is a 10 percent IRS penalty for distributions taken within the first five years or prior to age fifty-nine and a half.) There are methods of getting your money out early by borrowing the funds or if disabled or have a hardship situation, but for the most part money flowing into these plans should be regarded as retirement money that cannot be touched until then.

Various Types of Retirement Plans

Our intention here is not to give an in-depth description of every type of qualified plan available, but rather a brief description of each to help you understand basic terms and definitions associated with each different plan. Highlights of qualified plans include:

- Tax-deductible contributions
- Tax-deferred growth of investment earnings
- Most protected from claims of creditors

Some drawbacks of qualified plans include:

- Plan assets are generally illiquid until you reach age fifty-nine and a half. (10 percent IRS penalty applies to distributions prior to age fifty-nine and a half.)

- Annual contributions may be restrictive, in particular for the high-income specialist and practice owners.
- All distributions are taxed at ordinary income upon withdrawal.
- Complexity of plan design, setup, and administration can be high.

Here is a brief discussion of the various retirement plans.

Simple IRAs

A Simple IRA is generally a good option for a business with a small number of employees. A Simple IRA allows all employees to contribute a portion of their salary each paycheck, and will require that an employer contribution be made on behalf of all eligible employees. Current guidelines allow each employee to set aside up to $12,500 in 2016. Contributions made to the plan will be 100 percent tax-deductible. In addition, the employer or practice owner must *either* match employee contributions dollar for dollar up to 3 percent of an employee's compensation *or* make a contribution of 2 percent of compensation for all eligible employees, regardless of whether they are contributing their own money to the plan. Simple IRAs are easy to set up, very inexpensive to administer, and very attractive for smaller practices looking to offer a qualified retirement plan without a lot of cost or hassle.

401k Plans

With a 401k plan, employers may allow their employees to choose to defer up to $18,000 ($24,000 if age fifty or over) annually into the plan on a pre-tax basis (for 2016). In addition, the employer may elect to contribute a portion into the individual employee's account. For example, suppose an employee earning $60,000 of annual income contributes the full 15 percent into the plan and the employer makes a 3 percent matching contribution. The total contribution made into the plan would be $10,800 ($9,000 plus 3 percent of $60,000, or $1,800).

The employer may place a vesting schedule on the matching contributions. You would be required to remain with the employer a certain number of years for the matching contribution to "vest." A summary of 401k plan benefits include:

- High contribution limits for employer and employees
- A competitive plan to attract and retain key people
- Loan provisions for hardships and emergencies
- Flexibility with respect to matching contributions

Safe Harbor 401k Plans

A safe harbor 401k plan is intended to encourage plan participation among all employees and ease the administrative burden by eliminating IRS tests normally required with a traditional 401k plan. A safe harbor 401k plan allows employees to contribute a percentage of their pay into the plan. It then *requires* an employer contribution on behalf of all eligible employees, whether they are participating in the plan or not. This contribution is also always immediately vested. While there are several permitted matching formulas, an example would be 100 percent of participant contributions up to 3 percent of pay, plus an additional 50 percent of participant contributions up to the next 2 percent of pay.

Profit-Sharing Plans

Profit-sharing plans are designed to allow the employer to contribute to the plan on a discretionary basis. Depending on the terms of the plan, there is no set amount an employer needs to contribute each year. If contributions are made, you must have a set formula for determining how the contributions are allocated among all eligible plan participants. The maximum deductible contribution that can be made to a profit-sharing plan is 25 percent of eligible compensation, to a maximum of $53,000 in 2016. Eligible compensation is all the compensation an employer pays to eligible plan participants during the employer's tax year. Contributions are tax-deductible, and earnings accumulate on a tax-deferred basis. The employer takes the deduction for this contribution. The employer's contribution to each employee's account is not considered taxable income to the employees for the contribution year.

With a profit-sharing plan, the main benefit to the practice owner is the flexible nature of the contributions. It is possible to adjust contributions each year, depending on profitability of the practice, as long as contributions are frequent and ongoing. A real, tangible benefit of a profit-sharing plan for the employee is having contributions to the plan tied to the performance and overall profitability of the practice.

Money Purchase Plans

A money purchase plan is very similar to a profit-sharing plan in terms of contribution limits, benefits to employer and employee, setup and ongoing administrative costs, and eligibility. The primary difference is that employer contribution is a plan requirement. This amount is stated in the plan document. The benefit of a money purchase plan for the employer is that the fixed annual contributions to the plan make it easier to budget for and offers a measure of comfort and predictability for the employee. The inflexibility is often a big enough drawback that most practices gravitate to the other choices. It is beyond the scope of this text, but for certain situations (i.e., a small number of employees with one or two older and highly paid specialists), a money purchase plan and/or a variation of it can provide for sizable annual deferral limits that exceed the other plans.

Simplified Employee Pensions (SEP IRAs)

A SEP IRA is a retirement plan that looks much like a profit-sharing plan. The contribution limit is 25 percent of employee compensation up to a maximum of $53,000 in 2016. The administrative costs associated with an SEP IRA are very minimal, as are reporting and tax filing requirements. The plan must cover all employees who have worked for the practice in three of the past five years and are twenty-one years or older. SEP IRA plans are attractive for practices that have unpredictable cash flow, as contributions to the plan can vary or not be made at all, depending on profitability. The contributions are 100 percent employer-paid with no employee contributions allowed.

SEP IRAs can also be particularly attractive for someone who has a small side business that is run from their home. Contributions for self-employment income are based on net income, minus 50 percent of self-employment taxes paid and any deductible plan contributions or a maximum of $53,000. Since self-employment income is taxed very heavily, such a plan can be a very effective tool to lessen the tax burden. In addition, SEP plans provide creditor protection at both the federal and state level.

In summary, qualified plans are an integral part of your retirement, and there are many ways you can design a plan. When your income is at the highest tax bracket, we generally advocate taking full advantage of the plan available to you through your employer and contributing the maximum annual contribution limit allowable under current tax law. If you have just started work and have questions or concerns regarding the existing plan or a new plan, we encourage you to contact a competent financial advisor for several reasons:

- Your qualified plan will likely be your largest retirement asset, and as such should be carefully invested and monitored.

- Tax laws surrounding such plans have changed considerably and continue to change each year. This requires more time on your part to ensure that you have the most appropriate plan that provides you maximum benefit given your circumstances.
- Tax arbitrage planning opportunities exist. You should invest in a qualified plan at a high tax bracket and withdraw the funds at a lower bracket. So your retirement income will likely come from several sources as you design a retirement income strategy to maximize your after-tax income.

Calculating Your Tax Bracket

Just for you, we have taken the 10,000-page tax code and narrowed it down to two pages (see pages 61 and 62). Wouldn't that be nice if preparing our taxes was that easy! This is, of course, a basic guide only, just for education purposes, and doesn't factor in some of the specifics such as childcare, student loan interest deductions, moving expenses, and so on. But surprisingly, this is fairly accurate in estimating the federal tax liability.

We encourage working with your accountant, running one of the tax software packages, or simply using this guide any time you have a major change in your life that will affect your taxes. Family changes such as a birth, death, or marriage all affect the tax you owe. Financial changes such as a new job, a raise, going back to school, or buying or moving to a new house will also impact your tax liability, and a new calculation should be made. Compare your calculation to the amount you are having withheld from your paycheck, and if you are withholding too much, change this with your employer by filling out a new W-4 form.

This is especially useful for most everyone whose incomes adjust in accordance with their training. In July or August, you may start your employment and/or have a scheduled increase in your income or become a partner. If you don't work with your employer on the correct tax withholding, they will take out an amount that would correspond to you working for the whole year. Generally, there are many expenses, and having a higher take-home pay would most likely be more beneficial than getting a tax refund the following spring.

There are some important basic points to understand about taxes. First, getting a large refund isn't really all that smart. It means you just gave the government an interest-free loan for the year. If you are a terrible saver and use this as a forced savings plan, I'm guessing it still backfires on you because you know the lump-sum tax refund is coming and you have plans for spending that amount too! In any event, I suggest that you estimate your tax liability in advance and try to end up about even. That avoids any under-withholding penalties and any unexpected tax liability due that you may not be prepared for.

The second point is that it is always in your best interest to make more money. We've heard people say, "I just got a raise (or a bonus, or whatever), and it jumped me into the next tax bracket, so I'm going to take home less!" That's not how it works. The tax system is a progressive tax, and the more income you make, the more you take home. It's just that each additional dollar is taxed at a higher percentage, but the first dollars are taxed the same. Repeated, moving into a higher tax bracket affects the last of your dollars you earn, but the first dollars are still taxed at the same rate.

As an example, let's look at the Basic Federal Tax Estimator on the next page. Plug in your income (wages, interest income, etc.), and subtract contributions to pre-tax accounts to get your adjusted gross income. From that, you subtract your personal exemptions and either the standard deduction or your itemized deductions, whichever is higher. Then look up your tax bracket on the chart. The tax bracket is the tax on each additional dollar you earn, or the tax that is saved by virtue of reducing your taxable income by a dollar.

Suppose you are married and your taxable income happens to be $231,450. Your neighbor's taxable income comes in at $231,451, or $1 more. Bummer for them, right? Yes and no. Their tax liability is only 33 cents more than yours, because each new dollar is taxed at the 33 percent rate. They still have a take-home pay of 67 cents more than you, so while at a higher tax bracket, their take-home pay is more.

Your total tax is calculated as follows:

	The tax is:
First $18,550 of taxable income:	$1,855 (18,450 × .1)
$18,550 to $75,300 of taxable income:	$8,512.50 (56,750 × .15)
$75,300 to $151,900 of taxable income:	$19,150 (76,600 × .25)
$151,900 to $231,450 of taxable income:	$22,274 (79,550 × .28)
Total Federal Tax:	**$51,791.50**

Your friend's tax bill would be calculated the same as yours with another 33 cents of tax liability on the $1 above $231,450 at the 33 percent tax bracket. Work through your own situation a few times and this should be easier to understand.

Basic Federal Tax Estimator

This is a guide only, and is current as of 2016. For the most current tax law information, see www.basictaxestimator.com. This does not factor in childcare, student loan interest deductions, medical expenses, moving, and so on.

Gross Income (Wages, interest income, etc.) $_____

Minus: **Adjustments** (IRA, 401k, TSA, etc.) $_____

Equals: **Adjusted Gross Income** $_____

Minus: **Personal Exemptions** ($4,050 × # in household) $_____
(Phased out as income exceeds certain limits)

And the higher of:

Standard Deduction (Single: $6,300; Married: $12,600) $_____
Or

Itemized Deductions $_____

☐   State Income Tax
☐   Home Mortgage Interest and Property Tax
☐   Charitable Contributions

Equals: **Taxable Income** $_____

Federal Income Tax Due (See tax table below): $_____

2016 Individual Income Tax Rates

Single				Married Filing Jointly			
$0	to	$9,275	10%	$0	to	$18,550	10%
$9,275	to	$37,650	15%	$18,550	to	$75,300	15%
$37,650	to	$91,150	25%	$75,300	to	$151,900	25%
$91,150	to	$190,150	28%	$151,900	to	$231,450	28%
$190,150	to	$413,350	33%	$231,450	to	$413,350	33%
$413,350	to	$415,050	35%	$413,350	to	$466,950	35%
$415,050	+	No limit	39.6%	$466,950	+	No Limit	39.6%

There are substantial tax benefits with a variety of non-qualified investments also. The term "non-qualified" means there is no immediate tax deduction when contributing to these accounts, but the tax benefits can be more beneficial over your lifetime. The following assets are generally part of the *Capital Accumulation Stage*, but I'll provide the discussion of the tax reduction strategy of each technique in this chapter.

Stocks

As stocks appreciate in value (for this discussion, we'll assume they appreciate) there is no tax due on the appreciation until the stock is sold. Along the way, if any dividends are paid, the tax rate is less (20 percent for the highest tax bracket) than the ordinary income tax rate. In addition, when the stock is sold, if held for over a year, the gain is taxed at the lower 15 percent capital gain rate. So there is a benefit of tax deferral during the holding period and tax minimizing due to the gain being treated as a capital gain.

Roth IRAs

Assuming you have all of your *Security and Confidence Stage* issues taken care of, and your income is such that you can use Roth IRAs, I would recommend it. You do not get a current tax deduction, but under current law, all the growth (again, assuming it grows) is tax-deferred. Then, when you take the money out of the Roth IRA at retirement, you receive it income tax-free. Would you rather pay tax on the seeds going into the ground, or the end-of-year harvest? Growth in a Roth IRA may not be withdrawn until the later of reaching age fifty-nine and a half or maintaining your Roth IRA for a period of five years. Withdrawals prior to this (or if not held for five years) are subject to a 10 percent early withdrawal penalty.

Investors' anticipated tax bracket in retirement will determine whether or not a Roth IRA versus a traditional IRA will provide more money in retirement. Generally, investors who are in a higher tax bracket at retirement relative to their current tax bracket while making contributions to a Roth IRA benefit more than an investor who is in a lower tax bracket at retirement.

Real Estate

Real estate can be an excellent method of building wealth. Getting away from rent and into your first home is one obvious way. As for financing your house, contrary to popular belief, it can make sense to put little money down and stretch the mortgage out (and the tax deduction) in favor of freeing up cash flow for other goals and objectives. However, make sure you discuss your financing options with a mortgage specialist to determine what fits your situation best.

Life Insurance

In addition to the death benefit, cash value life insurance can provide tax advantages as well. As an accumulation tool, there is a cost for the insurance, so this is appropriate for someone who is younger and in good health and has a longer investment time horizon. The cash values grow tax-deferred and can be accessed income tax-free, if structured properly. It is generally best to avoid having the policy become a modified endowment policy. This occurs when too much money is contributed to a policy, and many favorable tax benefits are lost. Working with a very knowledgeable insurance or financial professional is a must if you are considering a policy as described here.

When you have a life insurance need, having a permanent life insurance policy can help you maximize your overall net worth in some other ways too. You reduce your need for term insurance, which frees up cash. In fact, the most beneficial time to have a permanent life insurance policy in place is at retirement because of all the advantages it provides. Briefly, you can be more aggressive in using and enjoying your other assets, because the life insurance essentially provides a "permission slip" to do so. Work with your financial advisor to coordinate this with your overall financial plan.

State-Sponsored 529 College Plans

There are a number of methods of putting investments in your children's or grandchildren's names. If the funds are ultimately to help them with their future college education expenses, a 529 Plan may be the answer. Some states allow a state tax deduction on the contributions, and all of the plans grow tax-deferred. If the funds are withdrawn for tuition, room and board, and "qualifying" education needs, the funds can be withdrawn tax-free also. These funds can even be transferred between family members. For a lengthier discussion, as well as a link to your state-sponsored plan, go to www.savingforcollege.com. However, make sure your own financial security is assured and your financial pyramid is sound before aggressively putting money into your children's accounts.

Annuities

An annuity is issued by an insurance company and is used for long-term retirement goals. There are numerous benefits of non-qualified annuities as another financial instrument. Namely, they grow tax-deferred, and for variable annuities you can switch between the separate accounts in a variable annuity without current income tax implications, and there are some death benefit guarantees to protect the value for your heirs. Annuities also generally provide options for guaranteed streams of income. Withdrawals from annuities prior to age fifty-nine and a half are subject to a 10 percent early withdrawal penalty, as well as potential deferred sales charges. You also will want to review the asset protection laws of your state to see if annuities are protected. They are in numerous states, thus increasing their attractiveness as an investment.

Variable life insurance, variable annuities, and mutual funds are sold only by prospectus. The prospectus contains important information about the product's charges and expenses, as well as the risks and other information associated with the product. You should carefully consider the risks and investment charges of a specific product before investing. You should always read the prospectus carefully before investing.

An annuity is a long-term, tax-deferred investment vehicle designed for retirement. If the annuity will fund an IRA or other tax-qualified plan, the tax deferral feature offers no additional value. They are not FDIC/NCUA insured, bank guaranteed, or insured by any federal government agency. Variable annuities have additional expenses such as mortality and expense risk, administrative charges, investment management fees, and rider fees. Variable annuities are subject to market fluctuation, investment risk, and loss of principal. The guarantees of a variable annuity are based on the claims-paying ability of the issuing life insurance company. The guarantees and the claims-paying ability do not have any bearing on the performance of the investment options within a variable annuity.

What percentage exposure you have to each type of asset category will depend on your time horizon, risk profile, and overall objectives. Once your allocation is established, regular monitoring and periodic rebalancing will be critical in accomplishing the two most important objectives: lower levels of short-term volatility and the highest possible long-term rate of return.

What Do You Do At Retirement?

Estimating your retirement needs is an important factor to consider at this stage of the pyramid. A financial planning rule of thumb is to figure on needing 70 to 80 percent of your pre-retirement income, although more people are enjoying a retirement lifestyle that is close to their working years. This figure should be based on the income you plan to be earning at retirement, not that which you're making today. To estimate this, look at your current expenses and subtract the expenses and savings that will not be needed at retirement, and add in extra expenses (travel, medical, etc.) that may be needed then. Consider the following:

- Will you still be paying a mortgage?
- Do you anticipate hefty medical expenses for yourself or your spouse?
- Do you wish to travel extensively?
- Will your day-to-day living expenses be similar to, or less than, what they are now?

If your budget allows, and you have your *Security and Confidence Stage* taken care of, take full advantage of any 401k or similar plans your employer offers, at least up until the amount the employer matches. This type of retirement investment defers tax payment on the contributed earnings until the money is withdrawn, usually at retirement. If your employer matches any of your contribution, this is an added tax benefit.

If you are self-employed, consider an SEP or Simple IRA retirement plan, which also allows you to take advantage of the pre-tax growth that has been described in this chapter. Deciding on the correct retirement plan will be something a competent financial advisor can help you with.

Universal Retirement Truths

Over the years, as retirement planning has become increasingly complicated, there are four simple truths behind any advice we offer on retirement planning, no matter how complicated the specific issue.

Start Early

The sooner you begin contributing to your retirement plan, the more time your money has to compound. You can always make adjustments to keep your investment allocation on track with your risk tolerance and time horizon profile. However, if you delay getting started entirely, it is very difficult to catch up.

Diversify

With regard to your retirement plan, after you have determined an appropriate investment allocation for your contributions, make sure you understand the investment objectives of each individual fund you are investing in.

Two funds with different names may have very similar investment objectives as well as holdings. Deferring into each fund will not give you the same degree of diversification as investing in two funds with different objectives.

We recommend you work with a financial professional to determine an appropriate asset allocation for your retirement assets and make sure you achieve a high level of diversification among the investment options.

Invest Consistently

Most plans allow for contributions to be made on a payroll deduction basis. This allows for contributions to be made to your investments every month. This eliminates any tendency to "time" the market and put larger contributions at the optimal share price. Regular investing over time is a proven method that "forces" you to buy more shares when the price of a fund is down, and fewer when prices are higher.

The goal of dollar cost averaging is to produce a lower average cost per share over time.

Hang Tough

If your retirement is still fifteen, twenty, even thirty years away, it is appropriate (even crucial) to construct a more aggressive investment allocation than that of an investment objective with a shorter time horizon. It is perfectly natural that such an investment allocation will experience higher levels of short-term fluctuation. This is necessary to potentially achieve a higher long-term rate of return.

As the time when you will begin drawing on this money draws nearer, it will be necessary to begin shifting a greater percentage of your assets towards investments geared more towards capital preservation. The time to worry about this is not during your peak earning years when retirement is still many years away. Ideally, at retirement, you have multiple income sources and are withdrawing money from your qualified plans to "fill up" your 15 percent bracket, and supplementing that with withdrawals from your non-qualified funds, Roth IRAs, and variable life policies for maximum tax leverage and efficiency. This is an area where the advice and wisdom of an experienced financial planner will be very valuable.

Financial Advisors do not provide specific tax/legal advice and this information should not be considered as such. You should always consult your tax/legal advisor regarding your own specific tax/legal situation

7

529 College Savings Plans

When it comes to planning for your children's future education costs, the 529 College Savings Plans have been designed specifically for this financial goal. From an investment standpoint, such plans enjoy tax-deferred growth of earnings, extremely generous contribution limits, and currently tax-free distributions of investment gains for all qualified education expenses. (We'll expand on qualified expenses in a moment.)

Our opinion is that the features that make such plans so attractive have less to do with their tax treatment and more to do with issues of control and flexibility.

Let's look at these plans from two difference perspectives:

- Investment and tax features
- Control and flexibility features

Tax and Investment Features

One frustrating aspect of investment planning from a tax perspective is that, when income increases beyond certain annual amounts, many investments that have attractive tax treatment become unavailable (Roth IRAs) or annual contribution limits become more restrictive as income goes up (401k plans). Neither of these is an issue with the 529 Plan. All investment earnings on the plan grow 100 percent tax-deferred, and the contribution limits are such that they would rarely be restrictive for the purpose of funding a child's education.

Contributions

Contributions to 529 plans are not tax-deductible but are considered gifts for federal and estate tax purposes. For the 2016 tax year, anyone may take advantage of the annual gift tax exclusion by contributing $14,000 per year ($28,000 for married couples) to any beneficiary. For financially independent veterinarians, there is a very unique rule for 529 Plans that allows for an individual to utilize five years worth of annual gift tax exclusion by contributing up to $70,000 ($140,000 for married couples) in one calendar year.

The limits imposed on 529 Plans are, generally speaking, so high that it is difficult to envision a scenario where it would become restrictive. The total limits outside of the above-discussed annual limits do vary a bit from state to state. Provided you get started early on planning for your children's or grandchildren's future education costs to take full advantage of the tax-deferred growth of investment earnings, such limits should not present a problem.

Distributions

Money has been contributed to a 529 Plan for the benefit of a child or grandchild, and the plan balance has grown significantly over the years. Now it is time to begin withdrawing the money to pay for college expenses, so what happens? When money is withdrawn from the account, it will be considered one of two things: a qualified distribution or a non-qualified distribution.

- Distributions that are utilized to pay for qualified expenses such as room, board, tuition, and certain other expenses will be considered qualified withdrawals, and as such are free of both federal and, currently, state income tax. For the parent with a long time horizon and children bound for academic greatness (and the accompanying price tag), there is potential to build up and withdraw all investment gains free of tax.

- Distributions that are utilized for anything other than a qualified expense will be considered a non-qualified distribution. The investment earnings will be taxed as ordinary income for the beneficiary and subject to a 10 percent penalty.

Control and Flexibility Features

The tax and investment features of 529 Plans are undeniably attractive and make such plans a very powerful financial tool for parents and grandparents who want to help with future educational needs. However, given the uncertainty of a young child's academic future, I often find reluctance among my clients to fund such vehicles for their child, who may or may not need the money. These uncertainties are very well addressed in 529 Plans.

Let's look at some of their benefits from a control and flexibility standpoint.

Who controls the account? The account owner controls the account. If your child reaches the age of majority in your home state, the 529 Plan balance does not become an asset of your child. You, as account owner, control how and when distributions are to be made.

Who can contribute to the account? Anyone may make contributions to the plan.

What happens if my child receives a scholarship or goes to a less expensive school? Perhaps one of the most attractive features of 529 Plans from a flexibility standpoint is the ability to change beneficiaries at any point. However, to avoid triggering penalty on investment earnings, the new beneficiary must be a family member of the previous beneficiary. The ability to move money in one designated 529 Plan to another child's plan, should he or she not go to school, attend a less expensive school, receive a scholarship, or any other reason, is a unique feature that gives parents a great deal of flexibility.

What happens if money is not used for college? If the money being withdrawn from a 529 Plan is being used for anything other than a qualified higher education expense, the investment earnings will be taxed at the beneficiaries' tax rate, plus a 10 percent penalty on earnings. Pulling money out of 529 Plans for non-qualified expenses should be avoided.

Must the beneficiary go to school in the state whose plan I used? No. Currently, all states recognize other state-sponsored 529 Plans, and as such, all distributions for qualified expenses will be both federally and state tax-exempt.

Funding Your Child's 529 College Savings Plan

With all the advantages of 529 Plans, the obvious question becomes, "How do we fund a plan for our child?"

When determining how to take full advantage of such plans, there are several assumptions you can predict with a fairly high degree of accuracy. Such factors include:

- Year in which your child enters college
- How many years (four or five) of post-secondary education you wish to be able to fund
- The average inflation-adjusted cost for both public and private education costs
- The percentage of the total cost you as a parent wish to be able to pay for

There are also many more variables you must simply make a best estimate for. A few of these factors include:

- The rate of inflation for college costs. College costs have experienced significant levels of increase over the years, and will likely continue to rise at a greater rate than the overall cost of living.
- The investment rate of return of the assets in the 529 Plan
- Where your child will attend school

All of these variables must be considered when determining how to fund your child's plan to arrive at the most important objective: having adequate funds available within the plan to be able to pay for the type of education, the length of education, and the location of the education you planned for. Any outcome other than this will result in one of two scenarios:

- *Not enough money saved up in the 529 Plan.* This will likely result in funds being withdrawn from other investment vehicles that have not grown tax-deferred and will likely not enjoy the tax benefits when withdrawn. As qualified distributions will be both state and federally tax-exempt, investment gains from other sources will likely be subject to tax. As discussed earlier, this is where an over-funded variable life insurance policy can come in very handy.
- *Too much money saved up in the 529 Plan.* The likely result of too much money in the plan will be excessive non-qualified distributions. While the earnings will be taxed at your child's rate and thus at a lower rate, this is only in the event that it is withdrawn for the benefit of the beneficiary. Should the money *not* be withdrawn for the benefit of your child, all investment earnings will taxed at *your* ordinary income rate plus a 10 percent penalty. So err on the conservative side and fund a 529 Plan at a level you feel comfortable with.

Our conclusion is that 529 College Savings Plans are excellent financial tools for the purpose of saving for future college costs. Like all aspects of your financial planning, regular monitoring is critical. As your child's academic greatness (hopefully!) begins to materialize, adjusting the contributions to the plan accordingly will ensure that the many benefits can be maximized.

A 529 Plan is a tax-advantaged investment program designed to help pay for qualified education costs. Participation in a 529 Plan does not guarantee that the contributions and investment returns will be adequate to cover higher education expenses. Contributors to the plan assume all investment risk, including the potential for loss of principal and any penalties for non-educational withdrawals.

Your state of residence may offer state tax advantages to residents who participate in the in-state plan. You may miss out on certain state tax advantages, should you choose another state's 529 Plan. Any state-based benefits should be one of many appropriately weighted factors to be considered in making an investment decision. You should consult your financial, tax, or other advisor to learn more about how state-based benefits (including any limitations) would apply to your specific circumstances. You may also wish to contact your home state's 529 Plan program administrator to learn more about the benefits that might be available to you by investing in the in-state plan.

8

Estate Planning with Asset Protection Strategies

This chapter was written by Robert Kaufer, an Attorney with Kaufer Law Firm, LLC. and has been included for educational purposes only. The applicability of many of the strategies discussed may be dependent upon the specific laws of states or countries in which the strategies are carried out. Financial Advisors do not provide specific tax or legal advice and this information should not be considered as such. You should always consult your tax and/ or legal advisor regarding your own specific situation.

Asset protection planning should not be viewed as a strategy to avoid paying legitimate and reasonable creditors, but as a process to protect your personal assets from unreasonable creditors. "Unreasonable creditors" are those who bring frivolous lawsuits or get unreasonable jury awards related to malpractice or personal liability claims such as automobile or slip-and-fall accidents. These unreasonable creditors do exist. They are the predators looking to sue anyone who is successful. It could be any legal action where a valid claim simply doesn't exist.

In general, asset protection is about putting up barriers in front of the unreasonable creditors to make it difficult or impossible for them to get your personal and business assets.

The key questions are:

1. What should I do?
2. When should I do it?
3. How far do I need to go?

What Should I Do?

The first step in navigating through the asset protection choices is to get educated. This chapter is not intended to be an exhaustive treatise on asset protection, but a primer to get you going in the right direction. It also is not intended to be legal advice and should not be taken as such. It is for information purposes only. Before implementing any asset protection strategy, you should consult with an attorney licensed to practice law.

Exempt Assets

The first line of defense against unreasonable creditors is the protection you get from the state you live in. Each state, through its statutes, exempts certain assets from creditors. These assets can include all or a portion of the following:

- *Home:* In many states, you get an exemption from creditors for your home. This, however, is usually not an unlimited exemption, and in some states (New Jersey, for example) there is no exemption at all. Other states (such as Florida) give an unlimited exemption, meaning a creditor cannot force you to sell your home to pay off a judgment, no matter what the value is. While these two states present both ends of the spectrum, the bulk of the states fall somewhere in between. An example is Minnesota, where the statute allows you to protect $390,000 of equity in your home. If the difference between your home's market value and all mortgages is greater than $390,000, a creditor can force you to sell your home, paying to the creditor any amount over the exemption.

- *Life Insurance:* Some states will protect life insurance partially or entirely. This can be both the cash value and/or death benefit.

  o States such as Texas protect all of the cash value paid into a life insurance contract. This means a creditor cannot force you to withdraw funds to pay off a debt.

  o To contrast the laws of Texas, Minnesota only protects death benefits of $46,000 if paid to the surviving spouse or child (the $46,000 exemption provided by this subdivision shall be increased by $11,500 for each dependent of the surviving spouse or child) and cash value of $9,200. Any amount above these can be reached by a creditor. Check with your local attorney in the event this has changed.

- *Annuities:* Annuities are similar to life insurance. Each state decides how much, if any, can be protected from creditors.

- *IRAs:* IRAs are also given a certain amount of protection by state laws, and the protection varies from state to state. Again, it can be all, nothing, or somewhere in between. The trend, however, is for greater protection to be given to these types of accounts. You should be aware that these laws are changing. In fact, Congress recently passed new bankruptcy legislation that included provisions for increased protection of traditional and Roth IRAs owned by a person in a bankruptcy proceeding.

- *ERISA-Governed Retirement Plans:* These plans are most commonly employer-sponsored profit-sharing/401k plans.

They are different from IRAs in that they are governed by federal law instead of state law. In most cases, federal law will trump state laws, including judgments that require an ERISA-governed plan to liquidate assets to pay a creditor.

An attorney licensed in your state should be contacted to determine what protections your state will give you against the unreasonable creditor.

Basic Estate Planning: Wills or Revocable Trusts

The foundation for any asset protection strategy is to have your basic estate plan in place. The two primary documents you can choose from for your basic estate plan are the will or the revocable living trust. While neither of these estate planning documents give much asset protection during your life, they can (if properly drafted) give good protection to your heirs.

The Will

Having a will does not avoid probate. It is an instruction manual to the probate court on how your probate-eligible property should be distributed, who should do it, and, if your children are under the age of majority, who should be their guardian. While you are alive, it does nothing to give you asset protection as you continue to own your property in your name. It may give some asset protection to your heirs, depending on the complexity of the planning.

The probate process is designed to be a creditor's forum. Any known creditors must be given notice, and there is a waiting period for creditors to stake their claim.

The Revocable Living Trust

A revocable living trust is an alternative to using a will for your primary estate planning documents. Having a properly funded revocable living trust will avoid probate. While it will avoid the probate process, it does not protect your assets from creditors. It can, however, if correctly drafted, give good asset protection for your heirs after your death.

The fact that the revocable living trust, if properly and completely funded, avoids the probate process and the creditor-friendly rules that come with it is reason enough to choose them over wills for your basic estate planning vehicles.

Family Limited Liability Companies and Family Limited Partnerships

One of the more common strategies used in asset protection to build upon the basic estate planning is the (family) limited liability company (FLLC) or (family) limited partnership (FLP).

FLLC

An LLC is a new form of business entity that has become increasingly popular. It combines the liability protection of a corporation with the tax and asset protection advantages of a general partnership. All fifty states have enacted LLC laws, with most of them looking and feeling like a general partnership. Some states (Minnesota, in particular) have taken on the feel of the corporation with the two levels of management (governor and manager). This feature makes it ideal for the FLLC, because it allows husband and wife to maintain various levels of control over the company depending on their life circumstances.

An LLC can elect to be taxed like a corporation or a partnership. However, the majority of LLCs today elect to be taxed like a partnership. That means these LLCs do not pay income tax. The income flows through directly to the members and is reported on their personal tax returns.

To begin the LLC, articles of organization are filed with the state in which you intend to set up the company. Some states (such as Minnesota) allow you to keep the names of the members, governors, and managers private with only the name of the organizer being filed (in most cases, the attorney who sets up the company). Having this anonymity can provide benefits and is an important component of an asset protection strategy.

FLP

General Partnerships

A general partnership is formed when two or more persons agree to carry on a business together to make a profit. It is as simple as that, and no writing has to be made and no documents need to be filed with the state except for registering the name to be used. It is good practice, however, for any partnership to have a written partnership agreement so all partners understand their rights and responsibilities. The problem with a general partnership is that all partners are jointly and separately liable for all debts of the partnership. The general partnership should be avoided at all costs because of this liability trap. If a partnership is to be used in an asset protection setting, it should be formed as a limited partnership.

Limited Partnerships

A limited partnership consists of one or more general partners and one or more limited partners. A general partner handles the control and management of the partnership. The tradeoff for this is that he or she has unlimited personal liability for all debts and obligations of the partnership. The limited partners cannot be involved in the control or management of the partnership, but they do enjoy protection from the debts of the partnership because their liability is limited to their investments in the entity. If a limited partner does participate in the control or management of the partnership, they may lose their limited liability.

Choosing Between the Two

For many years, the FLP was the entity of choice for asset protection and the minimization of estate taxes, but since its advent, the LLC is fast becoming the entity of choice because it is more flexible than the FLP and because there is no unlimited liability for the general partners as there is with an FLP. In a family LLC, the husband and wife can be involved in the management of the company without losing their liability shield while there are no creditors. If a lawsuit arises, the spouse/defendant resigns from their management role but retains their personal liability protection.

Creditor Cannot Reach Assets of an FLP or FLLC

In most states, the only remedy for a judgment creditor of an LLC or a limited partnership is a "charging order." A charging order is a legal remedy that gives the creditor the right to receive any distributions from an FLP or FLLC. It does not give the creditor the right to become an owner or the right to have a say in the management of the company. The creditor only receives the distributions intended to go to the owner/debtor. If this happens, the FLP/FLLC will simply choose not to make any distributions. The poison pill, however, is that even if the FLP/FLLC does not make a distribution, the creditor is responsible for the tax consequences as if a distribution had been made when the entity is taxed as a partnership.

The idea behind charging order protection is simple enough: owners should not be involuntarily forced into a partnership with somebody they do not choose. To get complete protection from this strategy, however, great care must be put into the "operating agreement" to give the maximum protection possible from creditors. Using this entity to hold the assets you most want to protect allows you to protect them from creditors.

It's important to understand that you must adhere to the business formalities of whatever business structure you establish. The risk is that if you don't, you may lose asset protection or estate planning benefits. Please consult an attorney.

Trusts

Irrevocable Trusts

In planning, it is important to keep the revocable living trust concept talked about separate from the irrevocable trust. The revocable living trust can be amended or revoked (you retain complete control as long as you are alive and competent), but it gives limited asset protection. On the other hand, the irrevocable trust will protect your assets (assuming the transfer of property was not a fraudulent conveyance), but you lose all control and benefit. In a properly executed asset protection strategy, they do play an important role.

One of the more common uses is to own life insurance. If the trust is created properly and all of the administrative formalities are followed, it will keep the proceeds out of a deceased person's estate for tax purposes and keep them away from creditors.

Asset Protection Trusts

A strategy that is gaining popularity is the asset protection trust (APT). An APT is a self-settled trust, meaning it is funded by the creator of the trust, who is also the beneficiary. This is different from the irrevocable trust discussed above, because in a traditional irrevocable trust, the intended beneficiary is usually the spouse or children and not the person who creates the trust.

There two main types of APTs: the domestic APT and the offshore (foreign) APT.

Domestic APT

In many states, the self-settled APT is not allowed. But in a minority of states, recent legislation is beginning to allow such asset protection vehicles. Eight states (Alaska, Delaware, Rhode Island, Missouri, Utah, Oklahoma, South Dakota, and Nevada) now allow some form of a self-settled trust to be set up that is outside the reach of creditors. These are very new and have yet to be challenged in court. Many legal scholars believe they are unconstitutional because of the "Full Faith and Credit" clause of the Constitution, which says, "A state is to recognize the judgment from another state." This sets up a conflict of state laws issue (the self-settled APT is exempt from judgment creditors in the state it was created) and the Constitution. This means the creditor must simply register the judgment and does not have to initiate the lawsuit all over again in that state.

Offshore APT

An offshore or foreign APT is similar to the domestic APT except the trust situs (location) is in a foreign jurisdiction. The Cook Islands or Nevis are two popular destinations. These trusts are self-settled, but the trustee is located in one of these foreign jurisdictions, thereby putting them out of reach of the U.S. courts. A creditor would not simply be able to register a U.S. judgment in one of these jurisdictions. They would have to initiate a new lawsuit.

While the trustee and trust may be outside the reach of the U.S. courts, the creator of the trust is not unless he or she leaves the country. Many state and federal judges despise this setup and will do whatever is in their power to unwind this type of trust, including putting the creator of the trust in jail for contempt of court. There is a long line of cases that deal with this issue, many not favorable to the debtor. These trusts are very expensive to set up and administer, and they should probably only be used in extreme cases and not with all assets. Consult with an expert asset protection attorney before considering these trusts.

When Should I Do It?

Time should be used as an ally. Having a plan in place and implemented for a period of time before an event (judgment or death) occurs will give the plan a better chance of withstanding an attack by a creditor or the IRS. If you wait until a lawsuit is initiated or even after an event occurs that may cause a lawsuit to be initiated, it may be too late because any transfer may be deemed a "fraudulent conveyance" and will likely quash any asset protection strategies you implement, on the theory that their only purpose was to deny creditors their claims.

How Far Do I Need to Go?

Assess your risk with the cost of implementing an asset protection plan and take the action that gives you the protection you're comfortable with. With that in mind, here are some planning rules of thumb.

Planning Rules of Thumb

The following rules of thumb are a guide to assist you in deciding if you need asset protection planning. However, the final decisions must weigh the risk of a lawsuit with the cost of the protection. In many cases, the tools referenced in this chapter make good sense for successful individuals, no matter the stage of his or her career.

1. *If you do not have children:* You may not need to undertake any estate planning at this time, but you should consult with an attorney in your area to make the final decision.

2. *If you have children:* You need to take some action to get the bare minimum for estate planning. You should be considering guardians for custody of your children and trustees to handle their finances if both parents die. If asset

protection concerns or will concern you, you best begin with revocable trusts. Another option is to use testamentary trusts inside of your will. Keep in mind these techniques alone do not provide asset protection for you, though they can provide protection to your heirs. These options are more expensive than basic wills, but it will be money well spent as these will be the foundation of your overall plan.

3. *Early in your career:* If you are just starting out, you most likely will have a low net worth and high debt load. Even though your net worth is relatively low, you should consider enlisting an attorney to help you decide whether wills or revocable trusts with pour-over wills are appropriate for your main estate planning tools.

4. *Business or practice owner:* If you have developed a successful business or practice and asset protection concerns you, you should look to implementing the following procedures if your state-given exemptions do not give you the protection you want and need:

     a. If you have substantial after-tax investments, including cash value life insurance, annuities, rental real estate, or recreational property, you should consider an FLLC.

     b. If you have an FLLC, use it for your cash value life insurance. Then you could use a separate irrevocable life insurance trust for your term insurance with total death benefits greater than $1.5 million to avoid estate taxes and protect the death benefits for your heirs.

Conclusion

If the intended goal of asset protection is to be completely judgment-proof, successful asset protection becomes extremely difficult. However, if the goal is to protect a portion of your estate against the unreasonable creditor, that goal can be obtained with the help of an experienced financial planner and attorney. Without successful asset protection planning, you will lose all assets that are not exempt if you get a judgment awarded against you. With the right planning, you will be able to build walls between you and your creditors that will improve your bargaining position and help you protect what you have worked so hard to earn.

Remember, you need to take action before there are any potential lawsuits against you. Otherwise, any actions taken may be unraveled by the courts.

As with every aspect of a financial plan, the estate planning and asset protection components are extensive and need to be coordinated by a professional advisor. The advisor should obviously be very knowledgeable, but also one who listens to you and your goals, and then communicates your options…so you can work together.

Please keep in mind that the primary reason to purchase a life insurance product is the death benefit. Life insurance products contain fees, such as mortality and expense charges, and may contain restrictions, such as surrender periods. Policy loans and withdrawals may create an adverse tax result in the event of a lapse or policy surrender, and will reduce both the cash value and death benefit.

9

The Speculation Stage

The Speculation Stage involves risking money you can afford to lose. Some people are never comfortable with this and thus should not consider it. These people should simply build their financial pyramid wider. This stage can involve different things for different people. It could be buying very speculative individual stocks or aggressive specialty mutual funds.

Subjecting your money where the principal has a high degree of volatility and risk has potentially high returns, but your money could also be lost completely. It is appropriate that this stage fits at the top of the pyramid, because if the money is lost, it won't be devastating to your overall financial plan.

Our rule of thumb when deciding how much to risk in a speculative venture is one year's worth of net worth growth. Never invest more than this! In a worst case scenario, if you lost the entire amount of your investment, you have basically lost one year's worth of financial progress. While not fun, it is not financially devastating. People get into trouble and can't recover financially when they take a lifetime's worth of savings and gamble with it.

As an example, let's say that your net worth is $100,000, and conservatively projected a year from now, it will be $110,000. This growth could be from additional savings, reducing debts, and/or growth from your existing assets. In any event, the $10,000 projected growth is the amount that could be considered for a very speculative investment.

In the event that an opportunity has come along that requires more than this amount, do not be tempted to risk more. Consider lowering your investment, delaying the timing until your net worth has grown, or involving a financial partner. The following ideas are just a few examples of possibilities that exist:

- Buying individual stocks of new companies
- Buying stock on margin (Be very careful!)
- Emerging Markets
- Specific Sector Investments

Again, keep in mind that speculative investments, while valid financial tools, are typically used only by extremely savvy investors and/or high net worth investors and institutions. They are not recommended to anyone who cannot afford to lose a substantial amount of their net worth. These investments carry an extraordinary amount of risk, and generally require intensive research and knowledge to carry out the investment.

In summary, no one has ever gotten into trouble financially by being too conservative for too long. Sure, there are some potential lost opportunity costs, but you can get into a lot of financial trouble by being too aggressive with too much money. That's why the financial pyramid is such a useful tool to help organize and prioritize these decisions.

You've worked hard to educate yourself in your field. We hope this book provides you with a framework to begin your financial plan, and that you achieve all of your goals and dreams.

10

Case Studies

Observations and Overview

In this chapter, we provide five specific case studies that demonstrate the concepts outlined in this book. We have provided a wide variety of examples to show that the pyramid of financial needs can be used in most circumstances as a method of organizing and prioritizing financial decisions. Hopefully, you can relate to one of these case studies and start applying the strategies to your situation. Please understand, though, each circumstance is unique and requires advice specific to their needs.

Of course, much of this is subjective, and ultimately the correct answer merges the quantitative and qualitative aspects of the decision into a financial plan you are comfortable with. We hope you find the following case studies to be a very helpful addition to the understanding of the techniques presented earlier in this book.

The case studies are titled as follows:

#1: Wrapping up Veterinary School
#2: Balancing Multiple Financial Goals
#3: Preparing to Buy Into the Practice
#4: Designing a Succession/Exit Plan

Case Study# 1: Wrapping up Veterinary School

Stacy is single and finishing up veterinary school. She will graduate in the spring and complete a one year equine internship.

She has a few financial goals at this time, including:

- Develop a budget to manage the low internship salary
- Understand and sign up for appropriate employee benefits
- Plan for purchasing another car
- Understand and manage her student loan debt
- Have a plan for emergencies and unexpected events.

The Numbers

Stacy will be living on $36,000/year or approximately $2,175/month take home. Her internship will offer a free place to live, a cell phone and use of a practice truck for ambulatory calls. Even though her parents offered to loan her money for a used car, as hers is starting to have mechanical problems, she has decided to use her car sparingly to see if she can get it through one more year. She has a job offer waiting for her when the internship is finished and will be able to afford modest car payments then. Stacy recognizes that some of her planning will have to wait for one year because of her small internship salary.

Her Net Worth Statement

Fixed Assets:

Savings Account:	$3,000
Checking Account:	$1,000
Money Market Account:	$0
Total Fixed Assets:	$4,000

Variable Assets:

Roth IRA:	$0
Mutual Funds:	$0
Total Variable Assets:	$0

Personal and Other Assets:

Vehicle:	$2,500
Personal Property:	$1,000
Total:	$3,500

Total Assets:	$7,500

Liabilities:

Credit Cards (21%):	$2,300
Student Loans (6.8%):	$110,000
Total Liabilities:	$112,300

Net Worth (Assets Minus Liabilities):	($104,800)

The Financial Plan

Security and Confidence Stage:

- Set up a money market mutual fund to use as her emergency reserve instead of the savings account.
- Focus on paying off the credit card debt with any extra monthly surplus cash flow.
- The practice will pay for a group disability policy, but her advisor has taught her that it won't cover her adequately, and she cannot take the policy with her when she leaves in one year. She will secure a private individual disability policy to insure her greatest asset: her ability to earn an income. This policy should protect her in her "own occupation", include a cost of living feature, and the maximum future purchase option allowing her to increase the coverage later without medical underwriting.
- Because of her tight cash flow, she will defer her student debt, and then next year, set up a repayment schedule for her student loans using the income based repayment (IBR) rules. She realizes interest will accrue this year, so she plans to pay at least $2,500 of interest per year when she starts her job, as that will be income tax deductible.
- Once she starts her job, she will secure an inexpensive term life insurance policy with conversion features, to lock in her insurability and set the stage to eventually supplement her retirement income.

Capital Accumulation Stage:

- Next year, Stacy should also start a monthly savings program that includes putting money into a mutual fund and a Roth IRA. The main objective here will be to just get started on learning how to track these accounts online, increasing her knowledge and confidence level.

Tax-Advantaged Stage:

- Since she is at the lowest income (and tax bracket) for her career, and she is not eligible to participate in the practice's 401(k) program, nor could she afford to contribute this year anyway, she should wait to contribute to a pre-tax retirement account.

Speculation Stage:

- Wait until the rest of the pyramid is more established.

Summary

Stacy is normally a saver. She looks forward to beginning her training so she can start earning an income, which will allow her to finish paying off her credit cards and begin building a savings and investment plan. She is happy that she has started educating herself to build the base of her financial plan, and is developing a trusting relationship with a financial planner.

Case Study #2: Balancing Multiple Financial Goals

Grant finished veterinary school seven years ago and has been working hard to pay off debt and get established in his practice, while balancing time with his family. His wife Morgan, a registered nurse by training, has been working part-time to stay home some with their two children, ages nine and six. The plan is for her to go back to work full-time when the youngest is in school full time next year.

They have many financial goals at this time, including:

- Buy a house in a few years.
- Continue to pay off their debts.
- Start to save for their children's education.
- Save for retirement.
- Reduce tax liability.
- Protect wealth.
- Have a plan for emergencies and unexpected events.

The Numbers

Grant works as an associate at a six-doctor small animal practice with an annual income of $115,000, which is a base salary plus production. He has access to a standard employee benefit package that includes health insurance, group disability insurance of 60 percent of income capped at $5,000 per month, and the ability to contribute to a 401k. Morgan's part time income is $48,000 annually. Their monthly take-home pay is $10,220, and their monthly expenses are $5,750, leaving $4,470 per month in excess funds with which to plan.

Their Net Worth Statement

Fixed Assets:

Savings Account:	$21,500
Checking Account:	$5,200
Whole Life Cash Value:	$8,800
Total Fixed Assets:	$35,500

Variable Assets:

Roth IRA:	$11,000
Mutual Funds:	$6,100
401(k) Balance:	$23,400
Total Variable Assets:	$40,500

Personal and Other Assets:

Vehicle:	$19,000
Personal Property:	$13,000
Total:	$32,000

Total Assets:	$108,000

Liabilities:

Vehicle Loan (6%):	$6,500
Credit Cards (17%):	$2,700
Student Loans (refinanced at 3.5%):	$63,000

Total Liabilities:	$72,200

Net Worth (Assets minus Liabilities):	$35,800

The Financial Plan

Security and Confidence Stage:
- Secure a personal disability policy on Grant to supplement the group coverage.
- Immediately pay off the credit card debt, and continue to focus on paying off the car loan (pay $2,000 per month toward this, and then save the extra when paid off, to be used for the new house.)
- Secure life insurance on Morgan using a combination of an indexed universal life policy and convertible term life insurance on both of them.
- Continue to stretch out the student loans for the length of the loan.
- Draft wills
- Add a $1M Umbrella Policy.

Capital Accumulation Stage:
- Commit to saving $2,500 per month into the following:
- Initiate 529 Plans for children's college fund.
- Initiate a fee-based brokerage account to start building a portfolio of non-qualified mutual funds.
- Fund the existing whole life and indexed universal life policies up to the limits allowed, being careful to avoid having the policies become modified endowment contracts. Convert the term life policies to variable life once Morgan returns to work full time.
- Consider buying their house sooner than later, to take advantage of today's lower interest rates, low down payment needed, appreciation the real estate market is boasting, and to allow enjoyment of the house with the family for more years.

Tax-Advantaged Stage:

- Maximize Grant's contribution into the 401(k) retirement plan ($18,000 per year); making sure this is actively managed using a carefully constructed portfolio.

Speculation Stage:

- Wait until the base of the pyramid is more established.

Summary

Their new plan takes care of "building a moat" around the financial castle they are starting to build. They feel more confident now that they have wills and appropriate levels of insurance. The life insurance plays an important role in the *Security and Confidence Stage* as well as the *Capital Accumulation Stage*, and was an excellent addition to the overall financial plan. With the risk management in order, they can aggressively begin a monthly savings plan for college and mid- to long-term financial security. In addition, they have a goal of rewarding themselves by meeting with a real estate agent to start looking for a home when the car and credit card debts are paid off, sooner than they had imagined. They finally feel like the "lean" years of veterinary and nursing schools are starting to pay off, and they feel much more educated about their financial goals.

Case Study #3: Preparing to Buy Into the Practice

Tamara finished her veterinary orthopedic residency eight years ago and has been diligently saving for her practice buy-in, a nice retirement, and a second home. Her husband Jack is much older than her, he is a self employed CPA and they don't plan on having children. Jack also has a small wine making business. The business does not generate a substantial income, but enough to fund trips and activities related to his business, and he enjoys this hobby.

They have many financial goals at this time, including:

- Fund practice buy-in.
- Buy a ski cabin in the next five years.
- Continue to help with her parents' living expenses
- Save for retirement.
- Reduce tax liability.
- Protect wealth.
- Have a plan for emergencies and unexpected events.

The Numbers

Tamara works for a busy specialty practice and is about to make partner. Her annual income prior to partnership is $164,000, and Jack's income is $135,000. Her anticipated first-year partner income is $240,000. She has access to the standard employee benefit package that includes health insurance, group disability insurance with a monthly benefit of 60 percent of income to a maximum $10,000 per month, life insurance in the amount of one times salary, and the ability to contribute to a 401(k) plan with an employer match to reach the annual maximum. Her current monthly take-home pay is $9,610, Jack's monthly take-home pay is $8,090 and their monthly expenses are $12,200 (which includes helping her parents), leaving $5,500 per month of surplus cash flow. However, when partnership income begins, the cash flow surplus is expected to be $9,323 per month.

Their Net Worth Statement

Fixed Assets:

Money Market Account:	$95,000
Checking Account:	$7,100
Fixed Life Cash Value:	$3,100
Total Fixed Assets:	$105,200

Variable Assets:

IRA:	$14,500
Roth IRA:	$17,750
Mutual Funds:	$7,000
Variable Life Cash Value:	$84,200
401(k):	$46,350
Total Variable Assets:	$169,800

Personal and Other Assets:

Home:	$500,000
Vehicles:	$38,000
Personal Property:	$120,000
Total:	$658,000

Total Assets: $933,000

Liabilities:

First Mortgage (30 years, 5%):	$365,750
Home Equity Line (3.8%):	$38,500
Student Loans (5.375%):	$91,000
Total Liabilities:	$495,250

Net Worth (Assets minus Liabilities): $437,750

The Financial Plan

Security and Confidence Stage:

- Increase umbrella liability insurance to $2 million.
- Increase the personal disability policy on Tamara to supplement the group coverage and accommodate her increased income once she is a partner.
- Significantly increase life insurance coverage for Tamara and Jack using a combination of heavily funded and minimally funded cash value policies and term insurance.
- Continue making regular payments on the mortgage and student loans. Once partnership income begins, may evaluate whether to accelerate some of the debt reduction, depending on the other goals and cash flow needs. For example, depending on the projected cost of the mountain cabin and prevailing interest rates, paying off a substantial amount of student debt will make more available for the down payment of the second home.
- Borrow money for practice buy-in on balloon loan, and deduct interest expense from K-1 income.
- Buy a long term care policy for Jack as he is approaching 50.
- Review wills, trusts, and appropriate estate planning documents drafted during residency in a different state.

Capital Accumulation Stage:

- The balance of the cash flow surplus, after making improvements in the insurance programs and adding the long term care policy noted above, should be committed to the following savings programs:
  - Initiate a fee-based brokerage account to start building a portfolio of non-qualified mutual funds.
  - Continue funding variable life policies to take advantage of tax-deferred accumulation of cash values under current laws, but keep in mind the

funding limits to avoid having a policy turn into a modified endowment contract.

- o Consider purchasing their ski cabin sooner than later, if interest rates are favorable, and the expenses can be worked into the budget. This enables the couple to enjoy more years in the cabin with their extended family, and depending on market conditions, may enjoy appreciation of higher property values.

Tax-Advantaged Stage:

- Continue to maximize the contribution into the 401(k) retirement plan, making sure this is actively managed using a carefully constructed portfolio.
- Resume Jack's contributions to his IRA and once he turns 50, using the catch up provision to maximally fund it.
- Maximize profit-sharing plan contribution. Coordinate the limit with the 401(k) plan. Use an actively managed account with a carefully constructed portfolio.

Speculation Stage:

- There is sufficient cash flow to consider more speculative investments once partnership income level is achieved, if this meets the client's investment objectives and risk/return tolerance.

Summary

Their new plan enhances their previous strategy and solidifies the base of their financial pyramid. They have confidence that the buy-in can be achieved, a sense of security that their ability to generate an income and protect one another and her dependent parents are ensured through higher amounts of disability and life insurance, their assets are protected with the increased liability umbrella, and clarity in the updated wills. The life insurance plays an important role in the *Security and Confidence Stage* as well as the *Capital Accumulation Stage*, and was an excellent addition to the overall financial plan. With the risk management in order, they can more aggressively save for retirement, and other mid- to long-term financial goals. In addition, they are considering purchasing the mountain home sooner than five years. They feel confident that the years of veterinary school, internship and residency are generating significant returns, and they feel secure in their financial future.

Case Study #4: Designing a Succession / Exit Plan

Roger opened his mixed animal veterinary practice 23 years ago, he added a partner 12 years ago. Janet has her teaching certificate and works with disabled children after being a stay at home mom for over 10 years. Over the past several years, a large portion of their disposable income has been allocated towards college expenses for their three children. During that time, most of their retirement savings have been cut back to a minimal level. Their youngest son will graduate from high school this year and begin college this fall, their middle child is in her second year of graduate school, and their oldest daughter is married, in veterinary school and expecting her first baby any day now. Roger and Janet have several financial priorities they want to address in the immediate and short-term future before they enter into retirement.

- Maintaining the college funding for the youngest child, help to pay some towards graduate school and veterinary school.
- Getting their plan back on track for retirement
- Structuring a savings plan that will allow them to maximize tax efficiency and tax deductions in their remaining working years
- Roger would like to retire in under eight years, but Janet would like to work a few years longer than Roger
- Coordinating a plan that will allow them to spend and enjoy their nest egg without fear of running out of money
- Explore how Roger will transition the practice ownership to an associate whom would like to partner and buy in
- Constructing an asset protection strategy to safeguard against potential any unexpected events

The Numbers:

Roger was originally the sole owner in this very busy small town mixed animal veterinary practice; he now has 1 partner and 3 associates, one of whom wishes to buy in. Janet has been working at the elementary school in the special education department. Their household income fluctuates between $300,000 and $350,000 depending on the revenue of the mixed animal practice. Roger's practice provides a group health insurance plan. His practice has sustained a group profit sharing plan that has been contributing seven percent of the employees' and his own salary at the end of every year. They have $10,000 per month after their monthly expenses to save for accomplishing their objectives.

Their Net Worth Statement:

Fixed Assets:

Savings Account:	$10,000
Money Market	$35,000
Checking Account:	$1,000
Total Fixed Assets:	$46,000

Variable Assets:

IRA:	$56,000
Profit Sharing	$413,000
Mutual Funds:	$200,000
Individual Stocks:	$182,000
Bonds	$95,000
Whole Life Cash Value:	$79,000
Total Variable Assets:	$1,025,000

Personal and Other Assets:

Home:	$610,000
Vehicles:	$30,000
Rental Properties	$220,000
Practice Building	$550,000
Total:	$1,410,000

Total Assets:	$2,481,000

Liabilities:

Mortgage	$0
Credit Cards (Pd. Off monthly)	$0
Total Liabilities:	$0

Net Worth (Assets minus Liabilities)	$2,481,000

The Financial Plan:

Security and Confidence Stage:

- Purchase an umbrella liability insurance of $3 million.
- Open an LLC for the rental properties and form a second LLC which will separate the ownership of the building the veterinary practice is in, with the intention of selling only his portion of the practice to a long time associate, while being able to collect passive rental income from the practice.
- Continue to maintain private disability coverage for Roger.
- Secure life insurance using a combination of over-funded variable policies and term insurance.
- Draft wills, trusts, and appropriate estate planning documents.
- Roger will work with their financial advisor, attorney, and the associate wishing to purchase into the practice, then build a succession plan. His advisor has suggested he get a complimentary informal practice valuation to get a ballpark idea on the value of his practice, until such time as his associate is ready to buy in - then they will get a formal valuation. Roger estimates it is worth $1.2M. His advisor will design a deferred compensation strategy for Roger and his partner to start immediately for this associate—to help fund a portion of this buy in.
- Roger and his current partner have not reviewed their Buy Sell Agreement in over 11 years. He was never made aware that a Buy Sell Agreement should be updated or properly funded, or even what that meant. Roger will work with his advisors to update his Buy Sell to reflect what the practice is worth today, and then explore how to protect each of the partners from premature disability or death.

Capital Accumulation Stage:

- Since the older children won't benefit much from the tax deferred compounding in a 529 plan, they should gift the low basis stock each year to each of them and have them sell it at their lower capital gains brackets.

- Use any cash and/or high basis stock to fund a 529 plan for their youngest child and use up to five years' worth of gift tax exclusions ($60,000) so that college is mostly funded at once.

- Initiate a fee-based brokerage account to start managing the mutual funds, stocks, and bonds.

- Heavily fund variable life policies, but keep them within the limits allowed by the IRS so that they don't turn into modified endowment contracts. This provides another opportunity for tax-favored growth with tax-free access to supplement retirement, while also addressing their life insurance needs.

Tax Advantaged Stage:

- Restructure the practice's retirement plan from a profit-sharing plan to a class allocation (profit sharing/401k plan). This new plan will allow a tax deductible contribution for Roger of $42,000 which is approximately twice the amount he was able to deduct in comparison to the old profit-sharing plan. The old plan required that all participants receive the same contribution, which restricted Roger from achieving the deductions he desired.

Speculation Stage:

- While Roger and Janet need to improve the base of their financial pyramid, they have already accumulated enough financial assets to allow themselves the option of speculating with a limited portion of those funds, if they are interested in doing so. They may begin to do this as they learn more about those options.

Summary:

Roger and Janet's new plan succeeds in placing a protection barrier between their personal and business assets so that all of their personal and business assets are protected in the event of a lawsuit. With a majority of the college funding taken care of after the stock sale, they feel that they are on track for retirement. They have the ability to focus their discretionary dollars into their retirement plan. Janet's additional income as a special education teacher has been helpful to supplement their savings program.

By revisiting the Buy Sell Agreement and placing proper funding strategies into place, Roger and his partner realize that their practice and its value is properly protected. By restructuring the profit-sharing/401k plan with Roger's practice, they were able to reduce their taxable income by doubling the amount he is able to contribute to the plan. By building a succession plan well in advance of the sale of his practice, Roger's associate will be set up nicely, and this creates incentive for her to stay and work diligently for Roger's practice. Roger will continue to practice veterinary medicine for several years and feels confident in his exit plan, where he used to wonder if and how he could exit the practice.

They are confident that their new financial strategy secures their future retirement plans, and they look forward to a time when they will be able to spend time with their young grandchildren, much more time with their extended families, and double the length of their vacations overseas.

ABOUT THE AUTHORS

Todd D. Bramson CFP®

Certified Financial Planner™ practitioner Todd D. Bramson has been working in the field of financial planning for over thirty-two years. He has been listed in the Top 150 Financial Advisors for Physicians by *Medical Economics* magazine in 2000-2009, 2012-2015, has contributed to many articles, and is an Editorial Consultant with that publication.

An exceptional teacher, as well as a motivating author and speaker, he has been quoted in numerous financial publications, and has spent several years as the financial expert on the local NBC live 5:00 p.m. news broadcast. In June of 2004, he spoke at the prestigious Million Dollar Round Table, a worldwide organization of the top five percent of all financial services professionals.

Mr. Bramson's belief, "If the trust is there, the miles don't matter," has earned him devoted clients not only in his hometown of Madison, Wisconsin, but in most states throughout the country. Along with all the designations expected of a trusted financial professional, he is committed to keeping abreast of all the developments in his field, and to playing an active role in his community. Todd is active in his community, The Evans Scholars Alumni Foundation, Blackhawk Country Club, and a director with Western Golf Association. He is also a member of Verandah Club in Fort Myers, FL and The Outpost Club.

Todd is also the founder and president of Bramson and Associates LLC. Information on his company, philosophy, and services can be found at www.toddbramson.com. He is also the author and creator of the *Real Life Financial Planning* book series, which now includes 11 books.

Darby Affeldt, DVM, Financial Advisor

Darby Affeldt, DVM is a Financial Advisor specializing in working with Veterinarians. As a Doctor of Veterinary Medicine herself, as well as a silent practice owner, she understands the complexities and needs of her clients. A lifelong entrepreneur, she is passionate about helping others succeed, and uses her personal experiences as a successful business owner to her clients to efficiently pursue their goals with financial peace of mind. Darby is deeply ardent when it comes to educating veterinarians to support them in achieving financial literacy.

Darby received her Bachelor's and DVM degrees from Colorado State University. Following her move to Seattle, she practiced as a relief veterinarian and simultaneously founded and operated a successful construction company, ultimately building over 100 new homes and one veterinary hospital. Darby was inspired to become a financial advisor learning from her previous experiences as a very busy business owner, without proper financial planning. She empowers her clients by offering a holistic, comprehensive, and educational approach to advising.

Darby has authored several articles, teaches at WSU College of Veterinary Medicine, and has spoken at veterinary symposiums. She is always interested in speaking to veterinary groups, and uses her impassioned humor to make finance fun and relevant. She co-founded C.P.R.-Comprehensive Practice Resoures. Outside of work, Darby is involved with Sierra Veterinary Medical Association, Vet Partners, Washington State Veterinary Medical Association, and started a low cost spay/neuter program at the Lewis County Animal Shelter in Centralia, WA.

Currently residing in both Seattle, and Olympia, WA, Darby is a two time Ironman finisher, enjoys cycling, swimming, snow and water skiing, traveling, and spending time with her family—husband, Christian Affeldt, DVM, and two adopted children, Emme and Truman.

Robert Kaufer

Robert Kaufer has over twelve years of experience as a practicing attorney working primarily in the areas of simple and complex estate planning, business and contract law, probate law, and residential real estate law. Bob received his law degree from Hamline University School of Law and an M.B.A. from the University of St. Thomas. He, his wife, and their two children reside in St. Paul. Bob's legal philosophy is to educate the client about their options and then help them make the best choices to meet their unique goals and objectives. Robert is not affiliated with CRI Securities or Securian Financial Services Inc.

Phone: 1-651-967-7932
Web site: www.kauferlaw.net

Todd D. Bramson, CFP®, ChFC, CLU
North Star Resource Group
2945 Triverton Pike Drive #200
Madison, WI 53711
(608) 271-3669 ext. 218
todd.bramson@northstarfinancial.com

Darby Affeldt, DVM
Financial Advisor
North Star Resource Group
1100 Dexter Ave N, Suite 100
Seattle, WA 98109
(206) 321-6566
Assistant: (602) 224-8002
Darby.Affeldt@northstarfinancial.com

Made in the USA
San Bernardino, CA
01 February 2016